Strange
Breeding Habits
of Aquarium Fish

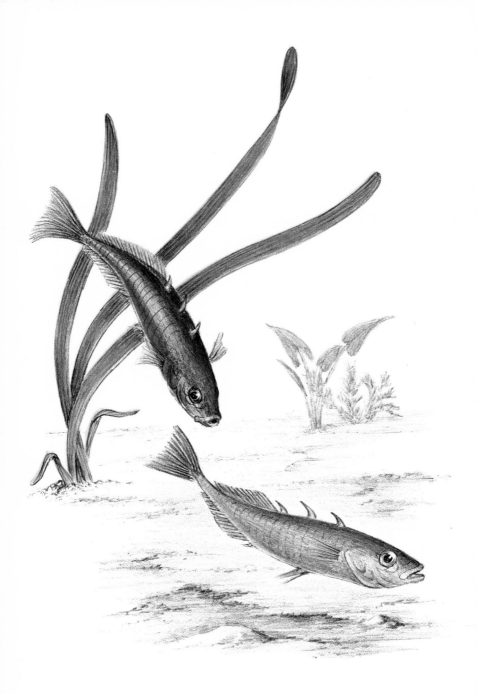

Strange Breeding Habits of Aquarium Fish

HILDA SIMON

Illustrated by the Author

DODD, MEAD & COMPANY New York

ISBN: 0-396-07025-6
Library of Congress Catalog Card Number: 74-11798
Printed in the United States of America

Acknowledgments

IN EVERY book about animals and their behavior, the task of gathering the information and doing the research—which includes observation of live animals—for both the text and the illustrations is formidable indeed, and could not be accomplished without the help of others. I acknowledge gratefully my indebtedness not only to ichthyologists such as Dr. Irenaeus Eibl-Eibesfeldt and Christopher W. Coates, and animal behavior experts such as Dr. Konrad Lorenz, but also—and especially—to such informed amateur naturalists as Dr. Leonard Breuer of Orangeburg, N.Y. Dr. Breuer gave me the benefit of his great knowledge on the subject of breeding and raising aquarium fish, collected over decades of devotion to this fascinating hobby. This was enhanced by his medical knowledge, which helped him to avoid or correct many of the common mistakes made by other amateur aquarists, and permitted him to breed successfully even difficult species.

I also take great pleasure in acknowledging the help

extended to me by Mr. Frank Rinaudo, owner of a pet store in New Paltz, who runs his establishment more along the lines of a small zoo with special attention to the welfare and comfort of his animals. Mr. Rinaudo's great interest in fish has led him to experiment with the raising and breeding of little-known and unusual species. He provided me with the opportunity to observe several of the species that are featured in this book, and to check details of behavior against information gained through his own experiences.

Last, but not least by any means, I wish to acknowledge the invaluable help given to me by Janine Gertner, librarian at the Museum of Natural History, whose patience and remarkable efficiency in locating hard-to-find research material made my work so much easier.

Because of the wealth of information available to me, I feel that both the text and the illustrations have benefited greatly, and I am indebted to all who have contributed toward bringing that about.

HILDA SIMON

Contents

Illustrations

Preface

THE GREAT popularity of keeping and raising fish in aquaria has over the years yielded a considerable amount of information on many such "pet" species. No one knows exactly where and when people started to keep fish in glass containers as a hobby, and just for their ornamental value and the pleasure derived from observing them. We do know that the Chinese were probably the first fish culturists, although they kept their fish in pools rather than in containers. Aquarium keeping did not become a hobby in the West until the eighteenth century, when goldfish were brought from China to Europe. Since that time, the number of aquarium enthusiasts all over the world has been steadily on the rise, and in recent decades, transportation of fish by plane has made possible the importation of new and formerly little-known species. Thus the small, more or less attractive and colorful fish suitable for home aquaria, and the important food fish necessary for commerce, were the two groups studied most closely in the past, each for very different reasons. In recent years, however, the growing interest in animal behavior has led to a tremendous increase in such studies of an ever-widening range of marine species, studies that are aided immeasurably by modern diving devices permitting scientists to remain underwater for long periods without awkward apparatus.

Fresh-water fish continue to be studied primarily in tanks by amateurs and scientists alike, for the two important prerequisites for underwater observations—good visibility and room to maneuver—are lacking in most fresh-water environments. Only in rare instances, and mainly in relatively shallow and fast-flowing streams and very clear lakes, has it been possible to observe certain fresh-water fish in their natural habitats.

The knowledge gained by studying fish in captivity is perfectly acceptable if we keep in mind at all times that the confined and artificial environment of the tank can lead to abnormal behavior in at least certain instances, and that caution is therefore indicated before proclaiming as typical for such species any behavior displayed by fish so confined. There is sufficient evidence that behavior representing a deviation from the normal habits of a particular species— cannibalism by usually protective parent fish, who devour their young in an aquarium, to give only one example—is a direct result of the fact that the natural environment of such fish has been insufficiently reproduced in the tank, and that they react with what we would call neurotic behavior.

Despite such drawbacks, however, observation and

study of fish in the controlled environment of the aquarium tank has many advantages. The combination of the increase in the number of aquarium devotees, the spread of sophisticated biological knowledge, and the diversity of fish available for the home aquarium has in the past few decades produced in-depth studies of species that otherwise would have remained practically unknown. Because the breeding of fish demands intimate knowledge of optimum conditions for normal courtship and mating activities, professional fish breeders, naturalists, and amateurs alike have spent—and will continue to spend in the future —a great amount of time and effort on such studies. It is only natural that fish with especially interesting breeding habits generate an enthusiasm that goes far beyond the pleasure derived from having colorful and attractive creatures displayed in a tank.

The same holds true for the salt-water species, most of which were little-known and rarely kept in home aquaria until quite recently, but which are now getting increased attention, mainly because of the growing general interest in the ocean and its life. Intensified underwater research by marine biologists such as Jacques Cousteau and Dr. Irenaeus Eibl-Eibesfeldt has yielded a large amount of fascinating new facts about the denizens of the oceans, and especially about the colorful inhabitants of the coral reefs. We have learned much about the territorial instincts, breeding habits, and survival tactics of a great number of species. With the aid of underwater films and photographs, we are getting captivating glimpses of underwater life, including such phenomena as the so-called cleaning symbiosis, which occurs mostly in the reefs, and involves certain species of usually small "cleaner" fish—such as the beautiful little neon gobies—that run regular cleaning stations to which the "client" fish flock in large numbers to be rid of irritating parasites or fungus growths. That the tiny cleaners appear to be immune to attack even when they enter the open mouth of one of their large and predacious clients to pick off parasites inside is only one of the still not fully explained wonders of that particular phenomenon.

In view of the steadily growing interest in the vast and colorful underwater world, it is to be expected that the future will yield many new and often surprising insights into the lives of fish and other aquatic creatures both in the ocean and in the fresh-water lakes and streams.

Strange
Breeding Habits
of Aquarium Fish

Chapter 1

THE MATING GAME

Intriguing Courtships

EVERYBODY IS familiar with expressions that use animals and their traits—or imputed traits—to describe human beings. Who among us has not employed such terms as "stubborn as a mule" or "sly as a fox" to characterize a person's behavior or peculiarities? When we stop to think about them, we find that many of these clichés are not particularly appropriate, especially when they concern animals that are not as familiar to us as the common domesticated kinds. For although mules, for example, are undoubtedly stubborn, a fox is not exceptionally sly or even wily, whereas a coyote might be thus described with some justification.

Most people would tend to consider the term "cold fish" highly suitable as applied to an unemotional and passionless person. After all, fish live in the water, are more or less mute, and unquestionably "cold-blooded"—a word that in colloquial usage has come to mean lacking all emotion and feeling, just as "hot-blooded" conjures up the image of an ardent, high-spirited, excitable creature. They would be wrong, however, for upon closer inspection the proverbial cold fish turns out to be an especially inappropriate term. As a matter of fact, it would not be easy to find—even among the higher animals—one that is more "hot-blooded" than certain fish during the pursuit of their courtship and mating activities. We have to recall only the incredible spawning runs of the salmon, in which these fish fight their way upstream for often hundreds of miles to their breeding places high in the cold mountain waters. They overcome—or die in the attempt to overcome—every one of the long list of formidable difficulties that stand in their way, including such all but insurmountable obstacles as waterfalls, until they attain their goal: that one brief moment of fulfillment when the female lays her eggs in the depression she scoops out in the gravel of the river bottom, and the male fertilizes them. Shortly thereafter, bruised and battered by their upstream odyssey, and spent by that final reproductive effort, the salmon die of exhaustion.

Any aquarium hobbyist of some experience knows from his own knowledge that some fish quite literally glow with passion during their courtship and mating rites, displaying hues of great depth and brilliance. Some normally plain and dull-colored fish may be transformed into gleaming jewels at such times. And for sheer poetry of sensuous motion, the love dance of the Siamese fighting fish can hardly be surpassed.

Prior to the recent surge of general interest in animal behavior, the only fishes whose habits had been closely studied were those from which man benefited in some way

—important food species such as the salmon, the trout, and the eel, or otherwise commercially profitable fish. High on the list are aquarium favorites, whose breeding and raising has become an industry as well as a hobby. Although the habits of relatively few species have been subjected to such in-depth studies, even a cursory glance at what we have learned about some of the others gives us fascinating glimpses of the variety and diversity of behavior found among this colorful group, of which the smaller species commonly kept in aquaria are of especial interest to most people.

There is, for example, the spraying characin, a member of a family that includes the feared piranha—probably the most rapacious of all fresh-water fishes—but is otherwise

A male spraying characin

made up of mostly small and peaceful species, many of which are familiar aquarium fish. The spraying characin is likewise peaceable as well as attractive, and its mating behavior makes it an unusually interesting aquarium inhabitant. During the mating ritual, the female jumps out of the water and onto leaves or stems of water plants that extend above the surface. There she deposits her eggs a few at a time, and is followed by the male, who also jumps out of the water to fertilize the eggs. In this unique but rather exhausting manner, the several hundred eggs a pair of this species commonly produces in a single spawning are laid and fertilized. The female's job is then done; the male, however, is far from having completed his part of the task. He remains near the eggs and guards them, even though they are above the water surface. To prevent their being dried out by the air, he sprays water over them from time to time with flips of his caudal fin. When the eggs finally hatch, the male directs a final, especially heavy spray at them, and so washes them down into the water. Only then is his task complete, and he goes about his own business without paying further attention to his offspring.

This strange behavior, which has given the species its common name, is unique even among the spraying characin's own immediate group; as far as we know, no other member of the family behaves in this manner. A closely related fish of the same genus, for instance, deposits its eggs in a pit dug in sand or gravel. We still have not found a really convincing reason why the spraying characin turns its spawning activities into such a difficult chore.

A South American suckermouth catfish

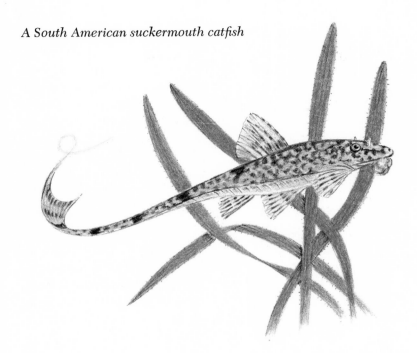

Another group with interesting habits that are still in-sufficiently explored is a family of small, peculiar catfish found only in South America. Unlike other small fish of this type, which are mostly omnivorous scavengers and often live in more or less stagnant waters, the suckermouth catfish of South America prefer fast-flowing streams and graze on algae, for they are completely vegetarian. They are distinguished by broad lips on the lower jaw, which aid them in grazing, and which, in at least one species we know of, play a role during the breeding cycle. The complicated courtship of these peculiar creatures has yet to be studied in detail, but we know that the eggs are deposited on previously cleaned surfaces such as a root or stone, and that the eggs, as well as the newly-hatched fry, are usually guarded by the male, although the female of one species carries the eggs on her large lower lip until they hatch.

It would be a mistake to assume that only the exotic species engage in unusual or remarkable behavior: some common fish of ponds, lakes, and streams of temperate regions, although frequently less colorful than their tropical relatives, have fascinating courtship, mating, and breeding habits. Cases in point are the sticklebacks and river bullheads, both of which will be described in later chapters. Another fish with interesting habits as well as beautiful coloring is the bitterling of Europe and eastern North America. This tiny relative of the carps is usually a rather undistinguished-looking greenish-yellow fish, but during the breeding season the male turns into a glittering golden creature whose metallic hues would make the traditional goldfish appear dull in comparison. The female during the breeding season develops a special tube-like ovipositor with which she injects her eggs into certain kinds of fresh-water mussels, where the male fertilizes them. The eggs do not seem to bother the mussel at all, nor do the young that hatch in the mantle of the mollusk and continue to live there, well protected from enemies, for several days. Finally, the mussel seems to get tired of its uninvited tenants and expels them with the waste water. By that time, the young are large enough to fend

Male bitterling displaying breeding colors

for themselves. Without the mussel, the bitterling could not breed. Again, no one so far has advanced a good explanation why this fish alone of all its relatives has evolved the pecular habit of selecting an involuntary baby-sitter for its young during the critical first few days of their lives.

Another rather ordinary-looking but intriguing little fish of temperate waters is the so-called dogfish of Central Europe (not to be confused with the small sharks known by the same name) which gets its name from its peculiar, paddling way of swimming. Although not too much is known about the courtship and mating habits of this fish,

A European "dogfish"

we know that the mother builds a nest in dense under-water vegetation, and later guards the eggs and young—in marked contrast to most other fish that practice brood care, where it is usually the male that has to bear the brunt of these tasks.

Although generally much less well-known and observed, the fish suitable for salt-water aquaria are every bit as interesting as the more familiar fresh-water species. Very few have so far been bred in captivity, but the fact that many instances of fascinating courtship and mating behavior are to be found among these fish is clear from what we have already learned about the few species that have been successfully bred, such as the fantastic sea horses, about which there will be more in a later chapter, or the neon gobies, mentioned earlier, which are distinguished not only by an attractive appearance, but also by their captivating ways. Fastidious and conscientious parents, a pair of neon gobies will spend much time on the selecting, cleaning, and preparing of the empty shell that serves them as nesting site. After the eggs are laid, the parents devotedly guard the nest, and inspect the eggs at regular intervals. Even after the tiny fry hatch, both father and mother continue to guard and protect them, in a display of parental devotion rare among fish, until the young are several weeks old. In addition to their interesting mating behavior, the fact that neon gobies act as cleaners for other, larger fish, whom they free of skin parasites and fungus growths, makes them fascinating and rewarding objects of observation.

Another intriguing species is the mudskipper, a fish related to the gobies, and found in brackish coastal waters, especially mangrove swamps, of the tropical regions of Africa and Asia. These fish have the unusual ability to sur-

A pair of neon gobies

vive outside the water for prolonged periods, and like to go on land and climb around on rocks and bushes. Their habit of skipping and crawling over the mud to reach a desired observation post from which they can survey their domain, has been responsible for their popular name. Mudskippers are peculiar-looking creatures with huge, protruding eyes, and are lively, entertaining, and quite pugnacious towards rivals. Very little is known about their habits, and they have not been bred successfully in captivity, but if their territorial fights, which are usually a preliminary to all courtship activity, are any yardstick, their mating behavior should prove most interesting, for the duels between the males are fought with great tenacity and violence.

Mudskipper "walking" on land

A rainbow wrasse

Then there are the wrasses, some of which go through the first part of their lives as sexually mature females, and later undergo a sex change that turns them into functional males. We know that in at least two species of wrasse, one female becomes a male upon the death of the last surviving male of any particular school. In that way, there is never any danger of the eggs not getting fertilized, because any female can turn into a male whenever it becomes necessary.

It is interesting to note that almost all fish with intricate and complex courtship habits also engage in some type of brood care, in which either one or both parents take part. There is a clear relationship between territorial fights, courtship rituals, and brood care in the majority of instances, and extreme territorial possessiveness usually indicates some advanced form of care for the young. By and large, the serious business of preparing a nest site for their future offspring is the first concern of the prospective par-

ent or parents after the territorial problem has been settled. Thus the love dance of the Siamese fighting fish is
preceded by the construction of the nest by the male, and
followed by his standing guard over the eggs and young.
The stickleback of temperate waters follows very much the
same sequence of procedure, although the two fish differ
considerably in mode and manner of their mating behavior.
In some species, a mated pair will form a true partnership,
and share in everything from preparing the nest site to
guarding and protecting the young until they can fend for
themselves. Often such a pair remains together in a lasting
attachment long after the breeding season.

It is interesting to note that in their breeding behavior
and especially in their brood care, such fish are reminiscent
of birds much more than of their much closer evolutionary
kin. No reptile, for example, practices any type of brood
care even remotely resembling that of the fish featured in
this book; the great majority, in fact, pay no attention at
all to their offspring once the eggs have been laid. The few
exceptions among reptiles that fashion a nest of sorts lose
all interest in their young once the eggs have hatched;
there is not a single known case where a reptile guards and
protects its young against enemies. The fierce protective-
ness of their nest and offspring displayed by many fish, on
the other hand, is strikingly like the parental devotion that
is a familiar feature of avian behavior.

In the chapters that follow, a few of the most outstand-
ing and interesting among those aquarium species whose

mating and breeding habits have been studied extensively
will be described. Their behavior should dispel once and
for all any notion that a fish is a "cold fish" when the time
for courtship arrives.

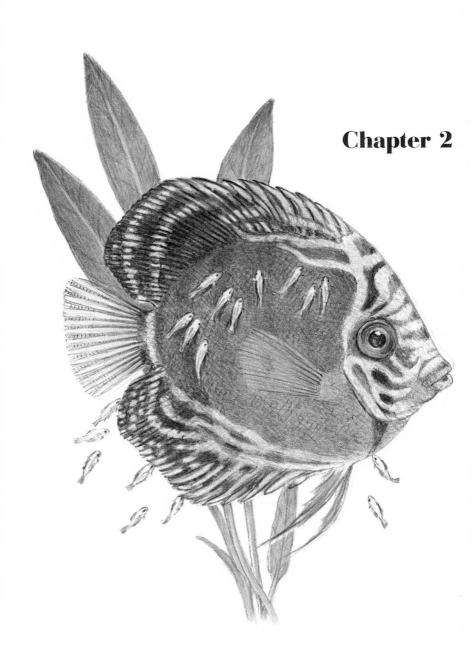

Chapter 2

DISCUS FISH

The Nursemaids

In THE LARGE, handsomely landscaped tank, the two fish hovered near each other, their eight-inch, almost disk-shaped bodies trembling and their fins spread wide as in barely suppressed excitement. Both displayed the same shade of deep, burnt-orange coloring that blended into brown on the back, with just a hint of darker vertical bars on the body, and a very dark stripe through the eyes, which gleamed brilliant red like rubies. On the head, the back, and the fins, irregular markings of an iridescent blue-green glittered as they caught the light, and stood out in sharp contrast to the overall warm hues of the body.

Neither the size nor the coloring of the two discus fish —aptly named because of their laterally compressed, almost pancake-flat bodies—gave any indication of their sex, nor was there any fin enlargement which in many other fish is the sign of the male. The female, however, was recognizable by her greater girth, which indicated that she was carrying eggs and ready to spawn. This distended abdomen of the female was the signal to which the male was responding. With a sudden turn, the suitor swam around the female until he faced her, and pressed his mouth against hers in what looked to all the world like a prolonged kiss. In reality, such lip-locking is not the show of affection that a human being would naturally interpret it, but rather a kind of pushing contest or tug-of-war that plays a part in various phases of pre-mating and courtship behavior observed in a number of aquarium fish.

As suddenly as it had begun, the mouth-to-mouth contact ended. The male continued to hover close to the female, however, and once again he spread his fins and began to tremble all over. At the same time, the color pattern of the body changed as the formerly indistinct vertical bars deepened into a dark brown, separating the basic orange-brown color so that the fish now appeared in a brown-and-orange-barred pattern that was clearly an indication of his emotional state, an invitation to the female to accept his proposal.

Nor did he ask in vain. The female quickly made up her mind to accept her suitor, and the couple interrupted their flirtations to get down to the serious business of selecting and preparing a good nesting site. Such a site had been provided by the owner of the aquarium, who had previously placed a smooth tile at an angle against the back wall of the tank near one of the corners. The tile was a substitute for the large smooth leaf or submerged branch which the discus fish would have selected in the waters of the Amazon region that form their native habitat.

It soon became clear that the tile found favor as an acceptable spawning site in the eyes of the prospective parents, for they began to systematically clean its already smooth surface to free it from any algae, fungus growths, or other possible impurities that could prove harmful to the eggs that were soon to be deposited on the tile. Fascinating to watch, this cleaning procedure is by no means limited to discus fish, but is found in a great many species, and especially among those living in stagnant waters.

Attractive and interesting as they are, discus fish are relatively new additions to the long list of traditional aquarium favorites. Only since the early thirties have these large and handsome members of the cichlid family been introduced to fish fanciers in the United States. Known variously as pompadour or discus fish, their spectacular appearance and unusual habits quickly made them favorites among aquarium devotees despite the considerable difficulties which were encountered during attempts to breed them and successfully raise the young. For although aquarists had considerable experience with other members of that family, the discus fish proved bafflingly different.

The *Cichlidae,* of which the discus is one of the largest species, are considered to be among the most advanced of fish, occupying a high position in evolutionary development within their class. Almost without exception, the several hundred species that make up this family have interesting habits. Most of them practice brood protection, although the type and extent of such "childcare" varies considerably among the different species.

Most cichlids are found in South and Central America and in Africa; only two species are known from Asia. In recent years, cichlids from Lake Nyasa have been imported as aquarium fish. These species are found nowhere else and are an excellent example of endemic evolution, for Lake Nyasa is very old and has been isolated from other bodies of water for a very long time.

No member of the family is much over a foot long; the majority range from between three and seven inches in length, although the dwarf cichlids measure only about two inches. Most are handsomely colored, and practically all can—and do—change their coloring to adapt to background and environmental hues, as well as to give expression to emotions and feelings.

Probably the most showy and therefore generally recognized cichlids are the famous angelfish, with their compressed bodies, very long dorsal and anal fins, and almost string-like ventral fins. Many other cichlids also have become aquarium favorites because of their attractive coloring and interesting habits. These unusual habits as well as their relatively high intelligence make these fish excellent subjects for scientific behavior studies. Individual differences have rendered such studies extremely rewarding; there are scientists who insist that cichlids are examples of fish capable of independent thought.

There are only two species of discus fish—although one of them has three subspecies—and the difference is mainly one of color and pattern, although the common discus is considerably larger than the very attractive blue discus

A handsome angelfish, or scalare

and its subspecies. The disk-shaped body of the common discus may attain a diameter of nine inches, but the width of a fish of that size does not exceed one and one-half inches at its widest part.

By nature, discus fish are shy creatures that like to hide until they get used to a new environment. Because they do not uproot and destroy water plants—a favorite pastime of many other cichlids—they can be kept in well-planted tanks that give them enough hiding places if they want them. Because of its intelligence, a discus fish may quickly get used to its owner, recognize him, and distinguish him from strangers, thereby showing a remarkable capacity for observation.

The breeding and raising of discus fish has presented aquarists with a formidable challenge, for they are not only

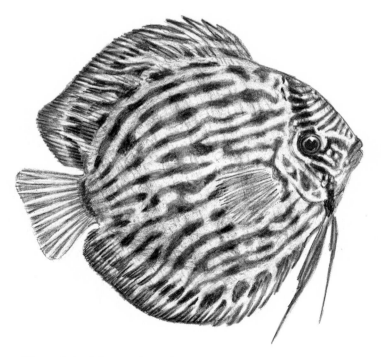

The original discus, Symphysodon discus

temperamental and nervous but highly unpredictable, especially during the courtship and breeding periods.

Probably the most frustrating of all the difficulties encountered with these fish was the aberrant behavior observed in many mated couples once the eggs had hatched, for time and again the adults turned on their own offspring and devoured them. These cannibalistic inclinations by fish belonging to a group renowned for the care they give to their offspring clearly indicated a breakdown of normal behavior—undoubtedly a result of the artificial conditions imposed upon the fish by the unnatural environment of the tank, in which some of the necessary ingredients for successful brooding and raising of the young were apparently missing. The solution to the problem was found through patient observation and experimentation until the fish were ready to accept the tank as a satisfactory substitute for home in every sense of the word. Although successful breeding of discus fish is still by no means easy, it has been done sufficiently often to be no longer considered the miraculous event it was up until quite recently. In order to follow the entire breeding cycle to its successful conclusion, we shall rejoin the mated pair of blue discus described at the beginning of this chapter.

After the tile had been meticulously cleaned—mostly by the female, with the male helping out but always on the alert to chase away intruders—the spawning runs began. While the male hovered at her tail, the female slowly moved over the surface of the tile, emitting a stream of tiny light-colored eggs from her ovipositor directly upon

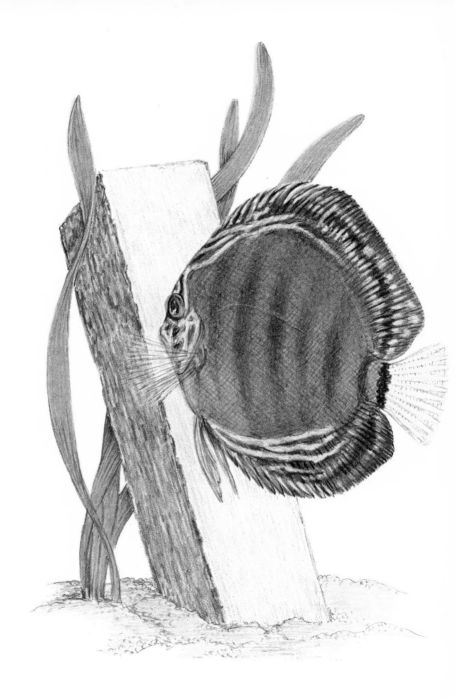

A pair of discus cleaning prospective nest site

the tile, to which the eggs clung as though glued to it. A few eggs refused to stick: the parents caught them up and spit them back among the others; those that still would not stick were eaten on the spot.

The female made several spawning runs; in each case, the male followed immediately behind and fertilized each batch with transparent, invisible milt as it was deposited. Now the waiting period began, and with it the parents' task of making sure that their prospective offspring would receive the best possible start in life.

In the days that followed, both parent fish spent a great deal of time with the eggs, fanning them with their fins. They took turns in this activity, which is designed to increase the oxygen content of the water around the eggs, and is typical of fish that live in oxygen-poor, more or less stagnant or slow-flowing waters. The eggs were also carefully inspected several times a day by the adults, and were frequently picked up and mouthed to make sure that no foreign substance or harmful growth adhered to them. The greater part of this job fell to the female, while the male hovered nearby to guard against any intruder or enemy with an appetite for discus caviar.

On the fourth day, the eggs began to hatch, and soon they were transformed into a wriggling mass of tiny fry. Almost transparent, with huge eyes, and heads that were still connected to the yolk sacs by slender, thread-like filaments, the young discus fish at that stage were still unable to swim. Not long after hatching, the parents came, scooped up their offspring by the mouthful, and transferred them to a new nesting site, which previously had been cleaned in the same meticulous manner as the first one. During the next few days, this process of shifting the young—which still could not swim on their own—from one site to another was repeated several times. The reason for this peculiar behavior is still not quite clear, but might very well be a part of the protective measures taken by the parents to discourage enemies from seeking out the young, and at the same time preventing harmful growths from developing at any one site.

The most exhausting part of the adults' job, however, begins with the moment when the young have used up all the nourishment in the yolk sacs and make their first efforts to swim and seek other food, for now the problem of keeping the brood together begins. As soon as even one of the tiny fish moves away from the brooding site, an anxious mother or father darts after it, picks up the youngster, and deposits it right back among the others. Very soon, this kind of babysitting becomes a time- and strength-consuming game for the parents as they dart back and forth after dozens of young they try to shepherd into remaining in one area. As more small fry join the breakaways, the task assumes impossible proportions, and is abandoned. At that point, however, the young school instinctively around the adults and stay close to them. As a matter of fact, they now begin to hitch rides on their parents' sides and backs, clinging to them like leeches. This is the truly unique phase of the discus' entire breeding cycle, for the young, which have been so carefully protected and guarded by their parents throughout their earliest development, now receive an additional and very unusual benefit in the form of a nutritious substance secreted by the skin glands of the adults, which provides the sole nourishment of the youngsters during that period of their growth.

This truly astonishing fact is a relatively new nugget of information about the habits of this handsome fish. It solved a mystery which had frustrated aquarists for some time. Because of the cannibalistic urges observed in many of the early captive mated couples, owners had sought the solution of the problem in separating the young from their parents and raising them in a special tank. This course of action, however, was not very successful either, for to their intense disappointment, the fish fanciers who tried it found that the young discus usually would not accept any of the tidbits offered to them—even though other young fish thrived on such food—and shortly starved to death. Finally, close observation of the few instances in which young were successfully raised in tanks with their parents provided the solution to the puzzle, for it became clear that the tiny fry clustering together on the adults' backs did so not just for the ride, but were in fact feeding on the mucus that thickly covered their parents' bodies.

This slime is normally found on the bodies of all healthy discus fish, and is a protective layer guarding the skin against a number of dangers which may include small lacerations, infections, and parasites. Removal of this slime will cause the fish to sicken and to die. Quite probably, the mucus contains certain ingredients that are toxic to

Adult discus with young feeding on its back

bacteria or parasites which would beset the discus fish in their environment.

During the breeding season, the normally transparent slime thickens until it becomes a whitish substance that obscures the color patterns of the adult fish. Although a detailed chemical analysis of the substance is yet to come, it appears from what we know now that the mucus is very similar in its chemical composition to the milk fed by the females of mammals to their young, for it contains fats, protein, and carbohydrates. It is thus quite clear why young discus fish that became separated from their parents soon after hatching starved to death: the "milk" secreted by the adults is prerequisite to the well-being and development of the youngsters. Up until quite recently, no one had been able to find a substitute food and successfully raise young discus that had not been "nursed" by their parents during the first few days after they started to swim. Now, however, several aquarists claim to have finally found a diet that can replace the nutritious mucus.

It is assumed that the secretion of this substance in breeding discus fish is controlled by hormones very similar to those that control lactation in mammals. The important difference is that both the female and the male discus secrete the "milk" needed by their offspring for normal development.

For the first week or so after they are free-swimming, the young discus fish live exclusively on the nourishment provided by their parents, and ignore all types of other

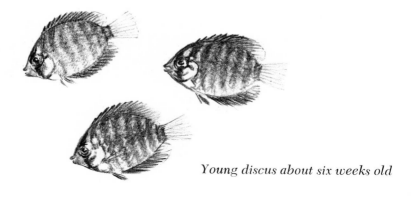

Young discus about six weeks old

food. They can be observed darting from one parent to another and clinging to them while they tear off and eat small pieces of the viscous skin secretion. At times, an adult may be all but covered by a mass of his tiny half-inch offspring, all busily feeding while saving energy by hitching a ride on mother's or father's steep flanks.

That the food provided by the adults is very nourishing can be seen from the rapid growth of the young during that first week or so. After that period, they are "weaned" —meaning that they accept other types of food and thus become increasingly independent of the adults. From that time on, the close relationship between parents and young begins to wane, and soon ceases altogether. At the same time, the consistency of the adults' skin secretions returns to its pre-breeding, less heavy, and more transparent condition. The young may now be removed to another tank and raised separately on conventional food without any harmful effects to their development. Within approximately six weeks, the grayish-brown, light-and-dark-banded youngsters are about two inches long, with nothing yet to indicate in their coloring the beauty of the adult fish. The parents, on the other hand, have returned to their normal everyday existence. The unusual and complex breeding cycle of the handsome discus with its unique "nursing" feature has been successfully completed.

In the two succeeding chapters, the advanced but individually different types of brood care observed in two other species of large cichlids will indicate the widely varying habits of this fascinating tropical group.

Chapter 3

JEWEL FISH

The Pugnacious Parents

THE TWO magnificently colored fish, their bright red bodies
and fins flecked with innumerable small, iridescent blue
and green spots, were stationed directly side by side over
a depression in the sand next to a large flat stone. Both
fish had a very similar appearance, but on closer inspection
the somewhat more intense colors of one, and the greater
girth of the other, identified them as mature male and
female individuals. They were, in fact, an "engaged" couple
on the brink of starting a family, and the hollow in the
sand with the adjacent stone was the nesting site, which
the two fish had just finished preparing and cleaning for
the eggs that were soon to come.

At that moment, another fish of almost the same size
and coloring approached the pair. It was another male
intent on winning the female away from her chosen partner even if it entailed a fight with a rival. However, the
newcomer had not reckoned with the ties that had developed between the engaged couple, which rushed to

meet him with a ferocity that left no doubt at all of their intention to kill the intruder rather than permit him to trespass on their nesting territory. The resident male opened the attack with a violent ramming blow to his rival's flank, and before the latter could recover sufficiently to launch a counterattack, the female assaulted the hapless intruder, who, not surprisingly, decided that a retreat into his own corner of the tank was the wisest course under the circumstances. As soon as he had left, the couple returned to their task of making final preparations for the arrival of their offspring.

In the entire cichlid family, there is probably no other species that surpasses the aggressively and pugnaciously devoted parenthood of the African cichlids known as jewel fish. There are two species, one of which grows to a length of ten inches and is found in Angola. This fish is rarely kept in aquaria, for it is so aggressive that it presents a problem. In a tank, it tears up all the plants, digs holes everywhere, and attacks anything and anyone regardless of size during the mating and breeding season. It is not surprising that this fish has been called the "wildcat among aquarium fish," a nickname it truly deserves.

The species described in this chapter is a much smaller fish that attains a maximum length of six inches but usually averages only four or five. In addition, it is much more colorful than its larger relative, and perhaps not quite so fierce, although the ruby cichlid, as it is also known, will unhesitatingly attack a man's hand lowered into the tank and bite hard to discourage any threat to the young.

Probably the most remarkable fact about the ruby cichlid, however, is the relationship of the mated couple, which comes as close to a "married life" in the full sense of the word as can be found among animals. The parents do everything together from preparing the nesting site to caring for the eggs and protecting the young. They share faithfully in all these tasks, and spend a large part of each day during the breeding season in activities designed to give their offspring the best possible start in life. Their "family sense" and the way in which the couple sticks together and shares the work is as remarkable as the fact that the mated pair later remains together far beyond the time needed to get the new generation started. This has led some observers to wonder whether these fish, as well as closely related species that behave in a similar fashion, may become attached to their mates as individuals—that is, recognize their partners, and react to the substitution of different males or females. Although observations so far have not been conclusive, there seems to be some evidence that individual attachment among mated couples of certain cichlids appears possible, and that one mate cannot simply be substituted for another individual of the same sex without provoking reactions of upset and rejection in the other mate. Be this as it may, the established mating behavior of these fish is remarkable enough to warrant special attention.

In order to observe the entire sequence without any disturbance, it is best to keep just one mated pair of ruby cichlids in a tank during breeding time, for although fas-

Two rival jewel fish fighting

cinating to watch, the battles fought by these fish are dis-
tracting and, if the combatants are not fully matched in
size and strength, may lead to injury of the smaller and
weaker individuals.

The initial courtship rites of a pair of jewel fish begin
with circling maneuvers during which the fish flare their
fins and their bodies tremble. This behavior is typical not
only of other cichlids but of a great number of other fish
also, although in most cases it is mainly the male that wants
to increase its size and look important by spreading its fins.
During the initial flirtation, the male jewel fish may change
color to a point where he appears almost blackish. Then
follows a lip-locking contest. Finally the female decides to
accept her suitor and follow him to the nesting hollow
which he has already excavated, usually near a large flat
stone. Now the prospective parents begin to clean the
surface of that stone meticulously and methodically, a
procedure typical for cichlids and many other species that
attach their eggs to stones and similar objects.

Usually, the jewel fish couple are extremely fussy about
this cleaning task. When they are finally satisfied, the female, hovering closely above the stone, lays her eggs in a
steady stream during each of several spawning runs. The
male follows immediately behind and fertilizes the eggs
that adhere to the surface of the stone. By the time the
job is finished, the entire top of the stone and sometimes its sides also are covered with a mass of tiny eggs,
for jewel fish produce them in great numbers during each
breeding season.

From the moment the eggs are laid, the nest is never again left unguarded. The parents share this guard duty faithfully: if one leaves to hunt for food, the other one stays behind until its mate returns to relieve it. This relief system is amazingly efficient—it evidently never happens that the parent on duty leaves before the other has returned, or that the one who is "off" fails to show up when the time has come for a changing of the guard. In this way, the eggs are never left unprotected, and the aggressiveness of the jewel fish parents guarantees that only a large or especially fearless enemy would venture to attack the nest successfully.

Even at that, however, guarding the eggs is only half the job; the other half, as with the discus and many other fish, consists of fanning them to insure a sufficient oxygen supply. For several days, the parents share these tasks while waiting for the eggs to hatch. When that happens, the parents almost immediately scoop up large mouthfuls of tiny wriggling fry still attached to their yolk sacs, and transfer them to a new, previously prepared and cleaned nesting site. Over the next few days, as the young gradually absorb the egg yolk, the parents again take turns in standing guard. Finally, the moment comes when the youngsters begin to swim on their own and look for the minuscule food they need during that initial period.

For the parents, a new but not less demanding phase of their child-care work begins at that point, for now the free-swimming young must not only be guarded and protected, but also strictly supervised and "educated." Again, both the mother and the father take an active part in this task, herding the youngsters about in a tight school and watching them like hawks so none can go astray. With one parent up front, the other bringing up the rear, and the young sandwiched in between, they look very much like finned versions of such birds as geese on a family outing. The most astonishing part of this child-care operation, however, takes place in the evening as soon as it begins to get dark, for at that time every night the young are "put to bed" by the parents. This may be taken quite literally, for the mother assumes a position directly above the nesting hollow and signals her chlidren to come. The gleaming iridescence of the female's heavily blue-dotted dorsal fin seems to play an important part in conveying the message to the young. By rapidly moving that fin up and down, the iridescent spots are made to gleam as they catch the light in what must be regarded as a kind of underwater version of signaling with mirrors.

As soon as they see this signal, the young unhesitatingly respond by gathering over the nest and locking their swim bladders through a muscle reflex. This causes them to become heavier than water, so that they immediately sink to the bottom of the nesting hollow, where they remain asleep—or at least motionless, for little is known about how fish sleep—throughout the night.

While the mother has in this way assembled most of the youngsters with the help of her special "mirror telegraph," the father has by no means been idle. His job is to search the tank for stragglers that went off on their own and did

not see—or heed—the mother's signal. As soon as he finds
such an adventurous youngster, the male scoops it up in
his mouth, swims back to the nest, and blows the tiny runaway down in among the others. Because the swim blad-
der of the young is so constructed that it locks the instant
the fish is inside the adult's mouth, it is already heavier
than water when the father spits it out, and immediately
sinks to the bottom into the nest. The male then goes off to
look for other strays, and does not relax until he is satisfied
that all youngsters are safely in the nesting hollow.

*Male jewel fish picking up one
of his stray youngsters*

That these highly intelligent fish are capable of a degree of thinking normally associated only with much higher animals is indicated by an observation made by Konrad Lorenz, famed naturalist and student of animal behavior. This charming tale is evidence of the unlimited surprises that await those who observe and study animals with love and understanding.

A pair of jewel fish guarding their young

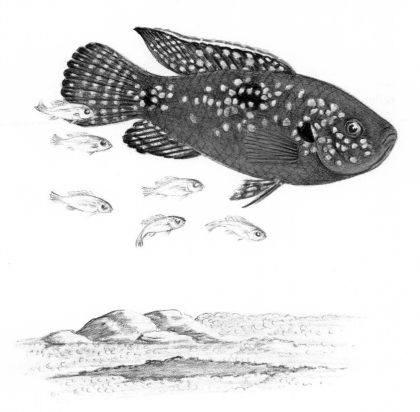

Dr. Lorenz at that time had a mated pair of jewel fish with a brood of free-swimming young. One day at dusk, he returned home and decided to give the adults an extra treat in the form of earthworms, which are one of their favorite foods. Most of the young were already lying in the nesting hollow, guarded by the mother, but the father was still on the prowl searching for stray children. At that point Dr. Lorenz threw a few earthworm pieces into the tank. The male was not far away and saw the food in the water. Very probably he was hungry, or else he was just tempted by a luscious-looking earthworm piece—in any case, he temporarily abandoned his search, swam over, snapped up the earthworm, and started to chew. Just as he was getting ready to swallow, he spied one of his runaway youngsters. Like a flash, he darted after it and picked it up. Now he had two objects in his mouth: one was a piece of food, the other, his child, and both were approximately the same size and shape. Dr. Lorenz watched with bated breath for what would come next, fairly sure that in this particular instance, devoted father though he was, the jewel fish could hardly help swallowing his offspring. Matters took an unexpected turn, however, when the fish remained motionless for what seemed a long moment of reflection. Dr. Lorenz maintains that the fish was thinking —really straining to find a way out of his dilemma. Then he made his decision. He spit out both his child and the earthworm, and watched as the two sank to the bottom of the tank. Then he carefully and closely inspected both objects, picked up the earthworm piece, and ate it without haste. After swallowing the morsel, he once more picked up his youngster, carried it back to mother and the nest, and deposited it among the others.

Dr. Lorenz reports that several of his students, who also had been watching, started to applaud as one.

Under normal conditions, several weeks pass and the young are quite large and well able to fend for themselves before the parents relax their solicitous attention. Even thereafter, a mated pair of jewel fish often remain together long after the breeding season and sometimes for life, in a monogamous attachment rare among fish.

Chapter 4

MOUTHBROODERS

The Fasting Mothers

THE LARGE tank was a teeming mass of tiny fry, each little
more than a quarter of an inch long. The large-eyed,
almost transparent youngsters were darting about in search
for minute food particles with quick, hasty movements.
Compared to them, the large fish swimming in their midst
appeared slow and deliberate in all its actions. A closer
look revealed a rather dull-colored, grayish fish with an
indistinct darker pattern on its sides and dark areas around
the eyes and mouth. About seven inches long, and massive-
looking because of its large head and thick lips, the fish
kept close to the main mass of small fry, almost as though
it was watching them. That, as a matter of fact, was
exactly what it was doing, for the fish was the mother and
sole guardian of the dozens of tiny youngsters in the tank,
and her guard duties left her very little time even for the
most elemental of all animal activities, the search for food.
Just as she spied a tasty morsel, a shadow fell across the
tank, and as on a given signal, her offspring came rushing

from all over the aquarium, headed for her wide-open mouth, and disappeared inside. It seemed almost impossible that there should be room for all, but appearance was misleading—not a single hatchling was left out, as the mother's cheeks and throat became more and more distended until they looked somewhat like the swollen pouches of a hamster who has been stuffing himself with grain. For a few minutes, the female kept her young inside her mouth while she reassured herself that whatever danger there had been was past. Then she opened her mouth wide and gently blew the youngsters out into the water, where they swam off quite unconcernedly to return to their search for food, but always ready, at the slightest indication of renewed danger, to dash back to the safety of mother's mouth.

Among the many different types of cichlids, the so-called mouthbrooders have been especially fascinating to students of animal behavior, and that is hardly surprising. The fact that they are hardy and easy to keep; the color

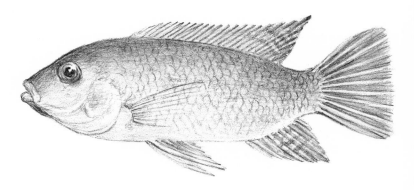

The black-chinned mouthbrooder, Tilapia macrocephala

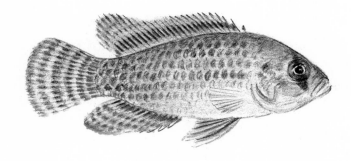

The small, handsome Egyptian mouthbrooder

changes many of them undergo during the mating season; the very special type of brood care they practice: all these factors combine to make them ideal subjects for study and observation.

Some species belonging to the group, such as the Mozambique mouthbrooder *Tilapia mossambica* described earlier, are among the very largest of the cichlids, attaining a length of more than a foot, although they are sexually mature at less than half that size, and may never grow to more than six or seven inches long. The black-chinned mouthbrooder *Tilapia macrocephala* is medium-sized, attaining a length of eight inches, while the small, attractively colored Egyptian mouthbrooder is only three inches long.

Although this group of cichlids is native to Africa, the Mozambique mouthbrooder was introduced into the ponds and rice paddies of Southeast Asia, where it has thrived and become a valuable food fish. It has also been used extensively for laboratory research by scientists, mostly in studies designed to find out more about the courtship and mating behavior. Interest centered especially upon the color changes that accompany such behavior, as distinguished from those that take place in the course of environmental adaptation. *Tilapia mossambica* has a very marked capacity for such adaptive changes. If given time —usually at least a few hours—a fish of this type may turn pale in a white-walled tank, and dark in a black-walled aquarium. It will also do its best to adapt to other colors: in an all-green tank, *Tilapia* will turn greenish, and brownish in a red-walled enclosure.

In contrast to the time it takes to change color for adaptive reasons, those that are based upon emotions are very rapid, a fact that is true of all fish as well as other animals capable of color changes. A Mozambique mouthbrooder displaying its neutral, grayish-brown coloration quickly develops a dark-barred or striped pattern if it is chased, frightened, or becomes excited. Should the disturbance continue, the pattern becomes a hatched design of crisscrossing bars and stripes. An interesting detail of this "fright" pattern is that a dark-colored fish has to pale in order to display it, whereas a light-colored fish has to darken. In physiological terms, this means that the emotion of fear triggers, within seconds, a response that concentrates or disperses pigment in the cells of certain surface tissue areas to form a definite pattern.

The third type of color change these fish are capable of differs from the others in that the changes are very slow,

Color changes of the male Tilapia mossambica

A pair of Mozambique mouthbrooders

are confined to the males, and appear only during the breeding season. Whereas emotional color changes are accomplished in a matter of seconds or minutes at the most, and the adaptive changes in a few hours, the individual phases of courtship coloration, which signal a male's getting ready to breed, and which are triggered by hormones, develop slowly over a period of days.

The beginning of the breeding cycle is heralded by the male's nest-digging activities. Around this time, his lips thicken considerably, and his color begins to darken on his head, fins, and breast. He becomes extremely aggressive, and defends his large, previously staked-out territory vigorously against intruders. In these fights, which may start with threat displays that include tail-wagging, fin-raising, and other movements designed to impress an opponent, each fish attempts to overwhelm its adversary with slaps of its caudal fins, and finally—if the rival persists—in mouthfighting in which the two combatants lock jaws in a vicious struggle. In many cases, the jaws of such fighting fish were found later to be dislocated, and in at least one observed fight, one of the rival males was killed within twenty minutes.

Once the resident male has established supremacy over his territory, he returns to the task of digging the deep pit in which the female will deposit her eggs for only a brief period. In some cases, the female may join her mate in the nest-digging. Then follows the courtship, which contains many of the elements that characterize the threat displays against rivals: fin-spreading and -raising, tail-wagging, and mouthdigging. The male then circles the female, taking care to show himself so she gets a lateral view and can be impressed by his size and coloring, which now is all dark. A male ready to breed displays either one of two patterns: an all-black, blue-banded coloring, or a velvety-black body with white cheeks and red-tipped caudal and dorsal fins.

After circling the female several times, the male tries to lead her to the nest, repeating his efforts until she follows him. As she enters the nesting hollow, the male again circles her several times while she deposits the eggs.

As soon as she is finished, the male descends into the pit to fertilize them; no sooner has he done that when the female collects the eggs in her mouth, and flees either into the school of other females or, if the tank contains only the one pair of fish, into a remote corner, for now she wants no further contact with the male. For his part, he ignores her, and may mate with several other females in the days that follow. It was observed in some studies that the female was so anxious to get the eggs that she did not even wait until the male had fertilized them in the nest, but gathered them up the moment she had laid them, and then followed the male to collect the milt he spread over the nesting cavity.

For the next two weeks, the female cannot eat at all, for she keeps the eggs in her mouth during this period. No matter how tasty a morsel of food may look, the female passes it up and refuses to break her fast in what to humans looks like heroic self-denial. An egg-carrying female can be easily distinguished by her swollen head and throat.

After about a week, the young hatch in the mother's bucal cavity, and begin to wriggle. However, they are still attached to their yolk sacs, and would be unable to swim on their own. When they attain that ability after a period of approximately two weeks, the mother opens her mouth and gently blows them out into the water. They are now sufficiently developed to swim about and seek the minuscule food on which they live. They do not, however, venture very far from mother, and at the slightest indication

Female mouthbrooder picking up eggs

of danger, they hurry back into the shelter of her mouth. Observations have shown that the dark eye and mouth region of the female helps to direct the young as they dash to her for safety.

After a period of three weeks, the formerly close bond between the now fast-growing young and the mother begins to weaken. Her exacting role of guardian is completed until the next breeding season. It is wise to remove the female from the breeding tank as the young become independent, for otherwise she may be tempted to look

upon them as delectable morsels of food rather than as her own dear children whom she has helped to raise.

In accordance with the fact that even closely related species show an infinite variety of behavior patterns, there are some mouthbrooding cichlids that have elected to place the burden of caring for the eggs on the male instead of on the female. Of the three best-known African mouthbrooders, two have assigned the main role to the female, whereas the third, known as the black-chinned mouthbrooder, features the male as the star performer. About thirty years ago, biologists working for the American Museum of Natural History in New York conducted a fascinating study of this species to find out just where and in

Female Mozambique mouthbrooder sheltering her young

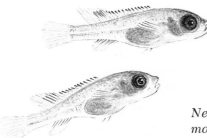

Newly-hatched Mozambique mouthbrooders

what way it deviated from the behavior of its closest relatives.

Placed into fifteen-gallon tanks, one pair to each tank, the first thing the fish made abundantly clear to their observers was the unwillingness of many to settle for partners selected at random for them by humans. Some of the paired fish fought so viciously that they had to be separated and permitted to choose other mates.

After a pair had established peaceful relations, normal courtship followed. The details were reminiscent of those practiced by other mouthbrooders, and featured much head-nodding, fin-raising, and spreading of gill covers. The courting pair also indulged in a good deal of tail-slapping and nipping, with the female being as active as the male in all these displays.

Finally, the couple interrupted its courtship, and began to scoop out a nesting pit. This was the first major deviation from their relatives' behavior, where the male usually digs the nest by himself. Both prospective parents were conscientious in their work, and carried larger pebbles a distance from the nest before dropping them. Later, they could be observed swimming head-down, almost vertically, and mouthing the bottom of the cavity, probably in an effort to remove anything that could prove harmful to the eggs.

Finally, the female swam slowly over the nest, and deposited a batch of some twenty large, golden-yellow eggs. The male followed and fertilized them, then turned around and sucked up the eggs in his mouth. He spent the next two weeks fasting, just like the females of his close relatives. Finally, the day came when he disgorged a teeming mass of fully formed, one-half-inch-long young into the water.

At that point, the biggest difference between the mouthbrooding fathers and the mouthbrooding mothers became evident, for instead of schooling about the parent whose mouth had sheltered them, the young *Tilapia macrocephala* fled to hide in crevices and among plants. Their instinct served them well, for the father immediately began to eat some of those that had not been quick enough to hide. It was clear that the weeks of protection and shelter provided for their offspring by the females of such species as *Tilapia mossambica* were considered an unnecessary luxury by the males of their closest relatives.

Whatever their individual peculiarities, the African mouthbrooders are among the most fascinating of all fish with specialized breeding habits, and well worth the attention of the student of animal behavior.

Chapter 5

BETTAS

The Veiled Fighters

HIS MAGNIFICENT veil-like fins flared and fully extended so they glittered in the same deep violet-blue as his body, the male betta circled about the small-finned and much less brightly-colored female, who seemed reluctant about accepting his advances. It was the male's third attempt at enticing her to follow him beneath the mass of frothy bubbles which he had assembled earlier beneath some floating vegetation in one corner of the tank. The first two times, she had fled from him and tried to hide in a clump of water plants on the far side; now, however, the male was no longer willing to be put off. His courtship grew ever more insistent, with frequent nudgings and nippings at the reluctant female's fins. Finally, she folded her fins and thereby signaled her willingness to accept her suitor's attentions, following him to the area immediately beneath the bubble nest.

Now began an exquisitely graceful water ballet ritual as the two bettas circled about one another, moving ever closer until the male enveloped the now-submissive female with his body in a U-shaped embrace. Very slowly, he turned her over on her back, and at that moment the female released her eggs, which her mate immediately fertilized. Then, being heavier than water, the eggs very slowly started to sink. At that moment, the male left the female, who continued to float on her side, inactive and in a torpor, and darted after the dropping eggs. Catching up as many as he could fit into his mouth, he carried them to the nest and stowed them away among the bubbles, quickly returning to reach the others before they sank to the gravelly bottom. Only after he had carefully inspected the gravel directly under the nest for any stray egg that was lying around did he consider his task finished.

Within the next few hours, the entire spawning cycle was repeated several times until the female finally had no more eggs. At that point, the hot-blooded lover of just a little while before underwent a complete and radical change: with surprising ferocity and violence, the male drove the female away from the nesting site. From now on, care and protection of the future offspring was his exclusive job; the female had done her part and was no longer needed or indeed wanted. In justice to the male, it must be noted that his actions are not a whim, for although some females may help with the egg-gathering, in most cases the mother tries to eat the eggs if she gets a chance. Knowing that the male's attacks might harm or even kill the female, the experienced aquarium owner removes her from the breeding tank and leaves the male in

Mating "dance" of bettas

Male betta dashing to pick up sinking eggs

sole possession of his nest and eggs. The courtship and mating drama of the bettas has come to a successful conclusion.

For more than one hundred and fifty years, the very special qualities of the fish that have become known and famed as the Siamese fighting fish have intrigued people all over the world, yet it was not their fascinating and complex mating rituals which focused attention upon them so much as the violent battles in which the males engage.

Bettas are members of the family *Anabantidae*, which derives from the Greek word *anabainein*, which means going up. One of the most famous of these fishes is an Indian species of the genus *Anabas*, called the climbing fish. This interesting little fellow is not only known to come up and out of the water; it also climbs trees and on occasion will travel overland for considerable distances.

Most of the other members of the group do not go as far as that particular species, but many are capable of surviving out of water for relatively long periods. The main reason for this ability is a special organ, the labyrinth— for which these fish are often known also as labyrinth fishes —which is a supplemental breathing organ. The labyrinth is a cavity that has a number of bony lamellae, and extracts oxygen from the air. The gills of anabantids are rather poorly developed, and would be incapable of supplying the fish with sufficient oxygen even in oxygen-rich water. However, most of them live in small ponds with warm, stagnant, oxygen-poor water. There the ability to come up to the surface for quick gulps of air, from which

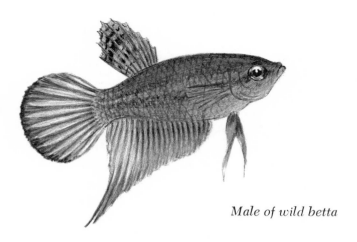

Male of wild betta

oxygen is extracted by the labyrinth, is a vital necessity.

The wild bettas are found in standing or slow-flowing waters of Malaysia and Thailand, including such small and shallow bodies of water as ditches and rice paddies. The wild form is an insignificant-looking brownish-green fish with relatively small fins that is a far cry indeed from the magnificent deep blue, green, or red veil-finned creatures we are used to seeing in home aquaria today. Only during fights and courtship rituals do the wild betta males display hues that convert the dull-colored fish into a scintillating mixture of red, green, blue, and black. As soon as the excitement fades, so do the colors. Comparing one of the original wild bettas with today's pure red or blue fish with their huge fins is like comparing an ordinary alley cat to a pure-bred angora. This applies mainly to the males—even today's aquarium-bred females are relatively dull-colored and small-finned.

Appearance and color aside, bettas have been prized for more than a century for their special fighting qualities. A hundred years before the first bettas were introduced into Western countries, people in Siam and adjacent regions were fascinated by the long-drawn-out and embittered battles fought among the males of this species. Fish fights were as much a sport in Siam as cock fights in other countries, and bets were laid on the outcome of the underwater contests, which in Siam had to be licensed for a fee that enriched the coffers of the royal treasury.

From various accounts, some of which date back about one hundred and thirty years, we have some good descriptions of the bettas used for the famous fish fights in Siam. Even then, there were considerable color variations in the color patterns and fin sizes of the wild fish, which fact foreshadowed the possibilities of the various color forms that aquarists later were able to produce by selectively breeding those fish with the largest fins and the brightest and purest colors. When bettas were introduced into the United States about sixty years ago, their handsome appearance and fascinating habits made them the favorites of many aquarists, and they still are among the top favorites today. Experiments with the breeding of new color variants are still going on today, one of the most coveted being the rare white, or albino, fighting fish, which so far has appeared only as a sport and has never been bred as a strain.

It was only natural that the curious fighting instinct of the bettas should have become the subject of intensive

studies by naturalists interested in animal behavior. In
itself, a display of aggressiveness and willingness to fight
during the mating season is nothing unusual among fish—
or most other animals, for that matter. However, the fighting spirit in the majority of fish seems tied in with the
breeding season, the urge to defend nesting territory,
mate, and offspring against the intrusion of rivals or
enemies. Sticklebacks, for example, will fight furiously and
to the death in the vicinity of their nesting sites, but removed from the nest, or outside the breeding season, their
fighting spirit is as diminished and subdued as their
normal coloring. With the bettas, however, this is not at all
true, for male bettas will fight at any time and apparently
without good reason, but only with males of their own
species. In the company of other fish, the betta is a peaceful fish that may get nudged away even by smaller fish in
a community tank. Show a male betta another male, however, and the fight is on. This peculiar instinct has given
naturalists a hard nut to crack, especially because the urge
to fight can be observed in very young bettas that are not
sexually mature. These pugnacious youngsters stage mock
battles among themselves despite the fact that they are
only a few weeks old and less than an inch in length. For
that reason, young male bettas have to be separated as
soon as they can be identified.

Because of the unusual habits of these fish, the courtship behavior was studied very closely, and was found to
be more interesting, and its pre-mating ritual more complex and intricate, than that of most other fish kept in

aquaria. During these studies, it was also discovered that the male betta recognizes individuals of the other sex mainly by their reactions to his threat displays. As soon as a male betta sees another betta, he flares his fins with a suddenness that reminds the observer of the opening of an umbrella. At the same time, his colors begin to glow, and he turns his side towards the other fish in a display designed to make himself look as big as possible. If the other betta is a female, she does exactly the opposite: she folds her fins, thereby announcing her sex unmistakably to the male and, if she is not ready to mate, immediately retreats. If, on the other hand, the stranger is another male, he returns the challenge by also flaring his fins and starting to change his color. Now the two males go through a ritual of challenge and threat and intimidation which may be compared to the ancient war dances of many tribes with which they not only attempted to inspire fear in the enemy, but also to muster courage and aggressiveness for an attack. Konrad Lorenz once compared this pre-fighting phase to the word duels of the ancient Greek heroes, in which they boasted of their own prowess while denigrating that of their opponents before entering into armed combat.

These threat displays of the fighting fish may last for a considerable period before the two adversaries decide to attack one another. When the attack occurs, it is a lightning thrust with wide-open mouth with which each fish tries to ram into the body of its rival. Soon the magnificent fins begin to show big tears and rips, and toward the end

Two male bettas in combat

of the fight they are usually badly tattered. Although their graceful shape, flowing, veil-like fins, and small size—some of the prize-winning bettas displayed at fish shows attain an overall length of five inches, but wild fish hardly ever grow to three inches long—make these fighters look less formidable than they are, bettas are quite capable of killing each other, and frequently do, although the reports of observers differ on that point. Usually, the weaker fish refuses to fight when he is badly battered and concedes victory to the stronger, even though the latter's fins also may be in shreds by the time that happens. Damage to the fins is in most cases reparable because they grow back within a period of several weeks, although scars may remain for life.

As mentioned earlier, the sequence of events is very different if the strange betta encountered by the mature male happens to be a female, especially a female ready for spawning. At that point, the male has already constructed the nest which will house the eggs, for like many other fish that practice brood care, bettas make serious attempts at mating only after they have everything ready and prepared for the future offspring. If during the nest-building activities a gravid female is nearby, the male will flirt with her, but refrain from actions that would lead to her spawning before the nest is finished and ready to receive the eggs.

The nest of the Siamese fighting fish consists entirely of air bubbles which the male blows into the water near the surface. He manufactures these bubbles by taking

large gulps of air, and then expelling that air in the form
of bubbles coated with a tough mucous slime. In time, the
nest, which looks somewhat like soap suds, may cover an
area six inches square and half an inch deep. Only after

*Three handsome bettas whose coloring resulted
from the crossing of various color mutants*

the nest appears satisfactory to the male does he proceed with serious courting.

If the female is willing and slowly approaches the male, he remains where he is, fins flared, gill covers spread, and his body trembling with anticipation. Then he slowly, and with exaggerated movements, swims off in the direction of the nest. If the female does not follow immediately, he returns, circles her again with trembling body and flared fins, and repeats his maneuver. Should the female continue to hesitate, the courtship starts to get rougher and stormier. Finally, she consents to follow the male to the area immediately beneath the bubble nest, and now begins the dance of love described at the beginning of the chapter. The highly ritualized movements of this minuet demand that the male always turn so he displays his side with a full view of his flared fins to the female, while she has to do exactly the opposite and move to constantly face him. The moment she deviates from this position, the male attacks her because of her "unfeminine" position. It is believed that displaying the side view means the challenge position of a rival to the male, and thus awakens the fighting instinct and provokes attack.

The assaults on the female by the male after completion of the spawning stem from an entirely different motive: now the male fears for the security of the eggs, and regards the female as just another intruder. After having tucked away all the eggs securely in the bubble nest, the father spends his time nearby, and keeps busy by repairing or enlarging the frothy mass of bubbles, moving the eggs about until he is satisfied they are placed right, and attacking anyone and anything that ventures close. There is great variation in the devotion of individual betta fathers to the welfare of their young, and the successful hatching of a brood depends very much on the qualities of the father.

Normally, the eggs begin to hatch about thirty-six hours after spawning. The hatchlings are tiny, and difficult to see, for they hang vertically suspended among the mass of bubbles with just their tails showing beneath. At that point, they cannot yet swim. The father watches them like a hawk and appears tireless in his guard duty. Whenever one of the youngsters drops out of the nest and sinks down, he darts over, picks up the tiny fish, and blows it right back among the bubbles.

Two days later, the young usually start to swim about slowly in a horizontal position. The father's task is now at an end; unlike males of some other species, he does not guard or protect them beyond this point. In the tank, he now has to be removed, for experience has shown that he will most likely soon regard his children as morsels of food. Evidently no instinct has been developed in the bettas that would inhibit them from such cannibalistic habits once their young have left the nest. Until the next breeding season, the male has fulfilled his duties, and can return to a normal and less demanding way of life.

Chapter 6

STICKLEBACKS
The Master Nest Builders

THE TWO SMALL fish kept circling one another like two
fighters in the ring, each waiting for an opportunity to
catch the other off guard. Both displayed their most brilliant breeding colors, the silvery hues of the sides and belly
offset by the green of the back and the deep, almost lumi-
nous red of the throat and breast. Finally, one of the tiny
combatants made a determined pass at the other, mouth
opened wide, his three sharp dorsal spines fully erect. His
adversary, however, adroitly avoided this thrust, and instead turned and came from below with an aggressive aim
at his opponent's belly. From that moment on, the changing, shifting colors of the two rival males gave evidence
of the ferocity with which the battle was fought, a ferocity
that foreshadowed the serious injury of one or both of the
dueling sticklebacks, so determined did they seem to
mortally wound each other.

At that point, the owner of the aquarium in which the
drama was taking place decided to interfere by removing

one of the fighting males. He knew from experience that the confined space of the tank—unless it happens to be a large one—tends to increase the ferocity and viciousness with which these territorial battles, which are usually a prelude to the sticklebacks' courtship and mating cycle, are fought by rival males if one trespasses upon the other's nesting site. Had the challenger not been removed in this instance, the battle could easily have ended in tragedy. The loser, badly or even fatally wounded, would have paled to a grayish-green hue, as though drained of his bright colors and his fighting spirit alike, and would have fled to a corner, there probably to succumb to his wounds. The winner, the deepening hues of his breeding colors proclaiming his victory, would have returned to his preparations for the construction of a nest, and the subsequent claiming of the females in the tank, while at the same time keeping a sharp eye out for any new intruders.

That was precisely what our remaining male, finding himself so suddenly deprived of his opponent, and therefore in full and undisputed possession of the tank's territory, proceeded to do. Over the next few days, he could be observed as he went through a fantastically complex, time-consuming, and exhausting string of activities whose only goal was to insure his future progeny a good and safe start in life.

Sticklebacks are a family of small fishes, none of whose members exceeds a length of seven inches, although most are much smaller, and the smallest species is barely two inches long. They have no scales, but are protected by rows of bony plates along the sides, and by a very tough skin that cannot easily be pierced even by a sharp instrument. Widely distributed in northern waters around the world, some sticklebacks live in fresh water, some in the

Male sticklebacks engaged in territorial fighting

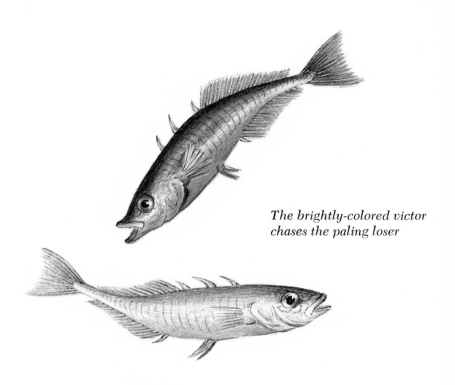

*The brightly-colored victor
chases the paling loser*

ocean, and still others—including the common three-spined
stickleback described earlier—are at home in either environment, and are often encountered in brackish water.
Although the various stickleback species differ both in size
and in coloring, the most common way of distinguishing
them is by the number of their spines. In addition to the
three-spined, the best-known are the tiny nine-spined and
the relatively large fifteen-spined stickleback. The latter is
a marine species occurring only in European waters. The
three-spined stickleback, which is found both in Europe
and in North America, seems to be an especially hardy fish

capable of surviving even in the uninviting depths of more or less stagnant waters—old moats, small ponds, and the like. This three-inch fish is undoubtedly one of the most handsomely colored of the group, although a color variant of the fifteen-spined stickleback caught along the coast of Sweden is reportedly even more strikingly colored.

Because of their attractive appearance and interesting habits, as well as their easy attainability, sticklebacks have long been favorites for the home aquarium, especially in Europe, and some enthusiasts have devoted themselves to the exclusive study of these small fish. Consequently, their life story and behavior have been much more closely observed by amateurs as well as by naturalists than those of most other small fish of temperate regions. They are indeed rewarding objects of observation, for they are active all day long, and not in the least shy or nervous. Unless the fish is sick or wounded, there is never a dull moment in the life of a stickleback, and it is almost impossible to get bored watching these little fish. High-spirited, curious, fearless, playful, quarrelsome, and always hungry, they provide a varied entertainment for the aquarium owner who supplies them with a reasonably suitable habitat. They are constantly on the go—or rather on the swim— chase each other, and seem to enjoy games of hide-and-seek. Despite all this activity, they keep a sharp eye out for —and immediately investigate—any movement indicative of something edible, whether that is a small snail making its laborious way over the sand, an insect that had the misfortune of falling into the water, or perhaps a smaller fish.

For that reason, it is not advisable to keep sticklebacks in a tank along with any other fish of appreciably smaller size. Larger fish do not bother them at all; apparently quite aware of their efficient weapons, sticklebacks do not fear larger fish, and are rarely attacked by them. Even such formidable predators as pikes, whose indiscriminate appetite is legendary, seem to have a healthy respect for the needle-sharp spines. The salmon is reputedly one of the very few fish that will unhesitatingly swallow a stickleback.

The most fascinating fact about the *Gasterosteidae* is one aspect of their breeding habits: the nest the male builds for the eggs. There are other fish that construct some type of nest, but no other species that fashions a nest so intricately woven that it looks like the handiwork of a talented weaver bird.

It all begins in the spring as the breeding season draws near. The male selects a suitable nesting site, and at that time his colors start to change and deepen, until they have acquired the characteristic bright hues. Soon, territorial fights between rival mates, such as were described earlier, follow as resident males are challenged by others. Once a nesting site has been selected, it is vigorously defended by its owner. Any male that comes close is considered an intruder, and if he decides to stand and fight, the battle is joined. A defeated male is pursued to the boundaries of the owner's territory and sometimes beyond, although the fighting instincts of the stickleback, unlike those of the betta, are in direct proportion to the proximity of his nesting site—the closer to the nest, the fiercer the battle will be. In many cases, both adversaries are finally too exhausted to go on fighting, and face each other near the border of their respective territories in what naturalists call threat displays. In such a threat display, the fish stands on its head, red underside turned towards the rival, and makes sudden darting motions as though it wanted to pick up something from the bottom.

Finally, however, territorial rights are settled and the resident male returns to his task of preparing the nest site.

Standing on his head, a male shows his red underside in a threat display

Depending upon the environment, the fish has selected a spot on sandy, pebbly, or even muddy ground but where the water either flows rapidly or at least is frequently agitated and therefore has the best available aeration. In a tank, he makes do with what he can find, just as he does in stagnant waters in the wild. All the same, a wise aquarist supplies him with a suitable, preferably sandy, well-aerated location where the layer of sand is deep enough to allow for the depression the male usually digs as a pre-

*Male stickleback gathers material
for the nest he is constructing*

liminary to the construction of the nest. By thus sinking the foundation of the nest below the level of the bottom, it can be better anchored as well as camouflaged.

During the excavation activity, the male's position is reminiscent of the threat displays against his rivals, and in fact naturalists assume that these displays are nothing more than a ritualization of the digging that has to be done for the nest cavity. Standing on his head, the male picks up one mouthful of sand after another, carries each load over to one side, and spits it out. This is repeated as many times as necessary to form a depression which the fish considers suitable. It has been observed that little or no excavating may be done by males who find convenient and secure anchoring and camouflage possibilities such as a submerged branch.

Now comes the task of preparing the foundation. The material, which consists of various plant parts, rootlets and similar fibers, is collected by the male without any assistance by any of the females, who pay no attention whatever to the structure that soon is to house their eggs. He tests each piece by releasing it to see whether it will float to the surface; those that do are discarded, those that sink are chosen as building material. Some of the long fibers used for the foundation provide the support for the rest of the structure. After the foundation has been prepared, it is weighted down with small stones or pebbles and then glued together with a kidney secretion discharged by the male during his work as he swims back and forth over the foundation. Now the nest walls, layer by interwoven layer, and each glued together, are built until the entire structure, closed at the top but with an entrance at one side, is completed.

Although the time needed for collecting the material and preparing the foundation may not amount to more than six or seven hours in most cases—always providing that a plentiful supply of suitable material is nearby—the process of completing the nest may take several days. Sticklebacks are meticulous builders, and some individuals are more fussy than others, and do not stop until all loose ends are tucked in or weighted down, and the tiny architect is finally satisfied with the size, shape, and appearance of his handiwork. Because of such individualism, as well as the differences dictated by the various habitats, stickleback nests built by members of the same species may vary a good deal both in size and appearance. Usually, however, the newly-finished nest of the three-spined stickleback has the shape of a slightly oval ball and the size of a small fist.

Once the nest is completed, the male wastes no more time in rounding up a gravid female, and, with a good deal of pushing, prodding, and tail-nipping, induces her to enter the nest. She remains only long enough to lay her eggs—usually no more than a few dozen—and then pushes her way out through the nest wall opposite the entrance, thereby creating a second opening, and swims off without another thought for the welfare of her offspring—the very epitome of thoroughly liberated womanhood.

In the days that follow, the male repeats his efforts with other females, and fertilizes each batch of eggs as they are

The female is nudged into the finished nest by the male

laid until a sizable pile has accumulated, or until he cannot find any more females that are ready to spawn. With the eggs safely inside, and the two openings at opposite ends of the nest insuring a constant flow of water, the first phase of the father's task to give the young a good start in life has been completed. Now, however, begins the most trying and exhausting part of his work: guarding and defending his future offspring against the countless dangers that normally lurk in the sticklebacks' underwater world. Enemies lusting for the eggs and the newly-hatched young include—besides other fish and numerous predatory aquatic insects typically found in such waters—especially the youngsters' own mothers, who, with a regrettable lack of the proverbial mother instinct, will use any chance to attack and eat their own young should the watchful father relax his guard even a little while. Of that, however, there is little to fear, for the male is a reliable and devoted sentinel.

As though this constant guard duty were not enough, the father has other chores to perform. Any damage to the nest while the eggs are still inside must be repaired, and the supply of oxygen necessary for the development of the eggs—especially acute in more or less stagnant waters— has to be replenished. By taking up a position directly in front of the nest entrance, and fanning water through the opening by rapid motion of his caudal fin, the male stickleback, like many other fish living in oxygen-poor waters, has found an effective way of providing the eggs with the life-giving element.

Finally, the day comes when the eggs begin to hatch, and another phase in the long process of raising a new generation is entered into by the male. After they hatch, the young fry soon destroy the nest almost completely as they search for the tiny aquatic creatures on which they feed in this stage, and the father now makes no further attempts to repair the damaged structure, which has served its purpose and is no longer needed. However, he does keep his brood together at the nest site, herding them like a faithful shepherd dog. His task of combination baby-sitter and watchman is not made easier by the natural curiosity of the hatchlings, nor by the determined attempts of the rapacious mothers and other enemies bent on catching a few of the youngsters for a quick lunch. Despite all these difficulties, the father in those first days never seems to slacken or tire in the performance of his duties.

Only as the young develop and grow does the male's attentiveness begin to wane, and proportionate to his offsprings' increasing ability to fend for themselves, the father loses interest in them and in the nesting site he has defended so long, and returns to his normal way of life. At that point, the brilliant breeding colors fade and are replaced by the duller hues of everyday existence. The most demanding, exhausting, and exciting time of the year is over, but only until the following spring, if the male survives until then.

Because sticklebacks lay fewer eggs than most other fish, the intensive care devoted to the protection and the raising of the offspring is vitally important to the survival

of the species. The fact that these small fish have done so well in holding their own without producing the huge masses of eggs with which most fish have to offset the depredations by enemies, attests to the efficiency of their

The young sticklebacks are guarded
by the father at the nesting site

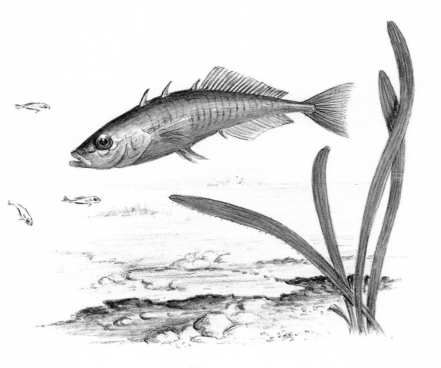

breeding methods, despite the mother's conspicuous lack of interest in her offspring. Through the father's care and watchfulness, however, each new generation of sticklebacks gets an incomparably better start in life than the unprotected broods of other fish living in the same environment, for large numbers of the latter fall prey, in the very first hours or days of their existence, to the countless enemies that lurk in the underwater jungle. Considering the marvelous care they receive when young, and the formidable weapons they have when adult, it is not so surprising that these small fish have survived in a variety of different habitats. Only in those waters that have been too heavily polluted by man in recent years have the sticklebacks succumbed, along with the rest of the underwater life, for no animal can protect itself against that most deadly of all threats to survival.

In the aquarium, the father stickleback naturally has a much less demanding job of keeping his eggs and young safe, for unless there are other, larger fish in the tank, which an aquarium owner would hardly permit during breeding time, the mothers are the only ones against whom the male has to guard the young. However, if the tank is large enough to accommodate several territories, attacks by rival males are common—including those by some lazy rascal of a male trying to dispossess the rightful owner of a finished nest, take it over, and thereby save himself the trouble of building one of his own. Such encounters are fascinating to watch, as are the tireless efforts of a father on guard duty to keep voracious females from getting at the eggs or the young. To anyone interested in animal behavior, these small, attractive, easily obtainable fish, even though they may lack the glamor of the exotic species, must count among the most captivating inhabitants of any aquarium.

Chapter 7

RIVER BULLHEADS

The Lazy Suitors

UNDER THE overhang of the curved flowerpot shard, the odd-looking wide head with its comical clown head and big eyes was just visible. The fish lay quite motionless, the rest of its body hidden in the darkness of the artificial cave, and watched intently the movements of a female, who slowly approached the half-hidden male as if curious to get a better look at him. She had come within a few inches of the cave opening when the male darted forward and locked his wide mouth over the female's much smaller head. After a moment, he released her briefly; instead of fleeing, she remained submissively on the spot with flattened fins, whereupon he again engulfed her head in his mouth and then slowly backed into the cave, drawing her with him. Once inside, he released the female, nodded his head energetically, and then made room for his bride by pressing himself into one corner of the cave. From that point on, observation of the events was somewhat obstructed by the darkness inside the cave, but the female soon was seen to investigate the nesting site, and especially the roof, even though she had to swim upside-down to do so. It did not take long for her to accept the cave as a suitable nest and deposit a batch of eggs in a corner against the roof. Shortly thereafter, she left, completely ignored by the male, who now gave all his attention to the eggs, which he had fertilized almost immediately after they had been laid. Positioning himself directly in front of the nest entrance, he began to fan the eggs with rapid movements of his fins. This was the beginning of a four-week period during which the male would spend the greatest part of his time attending his future offspring.

River bullheads are small fresh-water fish found in temperate zones in different parts of the world. The common species of northern Europe is some four or five inches long, and prefers brooks and streams with clear water and a rocky or gravelly bottom. Its normal coloring is a light yellowish- or brownish-gray with an indistinct mottled darker pattern. Its closest North American relative is the muddler, a fish similar to the river bullhead in size, coloring, and choice of habitat. Although little is known about the muddler's breeding behavior, it seems likely that these small fish would prove to be as interesting as their European cousins.

Next to the sticklebacks, the river bullhead is considered the European fresh-water species most remarkable for its highly specialized type of brood care. Even though it is nothing much to look at, its breeding habits have placed

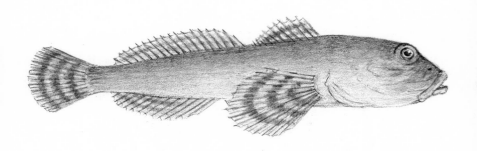

Male river bullhead in his normal coloring

the bullhead in a category of increased interest for students of animal behavior.

Because of its popular name, the fish has frequently been confused with the small catfish commonly known as bullheads in North America, and this confusion has led to a number of conflicting reports made even more perplexing by the fact that the American bullheads also practice brood care and guard both their eggs and young. Marine relatives of the bullhead catfish are known to be mouthbrooders with habits strikingly similar to those of the mouthbrooding cichlids. The male of the sea catfish, for instance, carries the eggs—and later the young—in his mouth for a period totaling more than two months. During this time, the father goes without food, and only after the young have become independent enough to leave the shelter of his mouth can he have his first meal after so many weeks of fasting.

The quickest way to distinguish the European bullhead

from its American namesake is by looking for the long,
whisker-like barbels that grow around the mouth of the
bullhead catfish. Size is an unreliable measuring stick, for
although the catfish is bigger, it is difficult to tell whether
an individual is full-grown.

Despite the fact that the river bullhead's breeding behavior shows some striking similarities to that of the
sticklebacks, they are totally different in almost every
other respect, including appearance and temperament.
The slender, colorful sticklebacks are active, restless, gre-
garious creatures that like to be on the prowl constantly,
exploring this or that or hunting for prey. Bullheads, on
the other hand, are solitary, bottom-dwelling loners that
like to hide, and spend much of their time lurking under
stones and in crevices waiting for prey to pass by. Then
they dart out with considerable speed and agility to grab
and swallow the hapless victim. Their menu includes
many different aquatic creatures from dragonfly larvae to
small fish—anything, in fact, that can be gulped down. In
contrast to American bullheads which, like most other catfish, are at least partly scavengers, river bullheads seem to
be partial to live and moving food.

The breeding season heralds great changes in the normal living habits of these loners, for it is the only time of
the year when they are in close contact with others of
their kind—and that contact is mainly hostile, except for
the brief courtship and mating period that brings male
and female together.

As with most fish that practice brood care, preparing the

nesting site is the first order of business for the male. Unlike sticklebacks, bullheads do not fashion their nest from material they gather; instead, they use a natural crevice or hole under a stone, which they enlarge and shape by digging to fit their needs. Because these activities are difficult to follow in their natural habitat, we have to rely for details on observations of captive bullheads in an aquarium.

These fish were given an artificial "cave" fashioned from large, curved pieces of stone or broken flowerpot firmly anchored in the sand and gravel of the bottom. The pieces were placed to make a slightly arched enclosure that left a wide but very low entrance at one side, for experiments had shown that river bullheads prefer the entrance gap between the roof and floor of their prospective nest to be very narrow, so they can do their own enlarging and shaping. After a site has been selected, the male wriggles head-first and with wide-open mouth into the sand at the entrance. When he has scooped up all he can hold, he swims off with his load and spits it out some distance from the nest. Pebbles and other debris are also

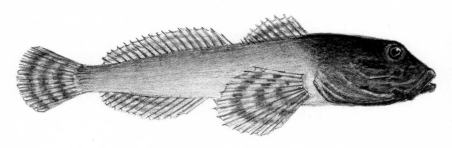

During the mating season, the head of the male turns dark

picked up and dumped, as are pests such as inedible crustaceans.

Once the entrance has been enlarged and shaped, the bullhead moves to hollow out a suitable depression inside his cave. Backing tail-first into the space under the stone, he moves his tail so rapidly from side to side that he may disappear temporarily in the cloud of sand he is dislodging. Finally, remodeling ends as the roof of the nest is examined and cleaned to make sure it is ready for the eggs, and the male takes up his waiting position, with only his head protruding from the entrance.

Should a rival appear on the scene during the nest-digging activity, a viciously-fought battle will ensue. The defending male's head turns black with excitement during these contests. Before a battle is joined, the males usually engage in threat displays designed to scare off the opponent. These displays include fin-spreading, raising of gill covers until the head appears twice as wide, and opening the mouth as in an attack. Only if these threats fail will the fight begin in earnest.

However, at the height of the breeding season and as the moment for enticing a female into entering the nest draws near, the aggressiveness of the resident male increases. At this point, his head may remain blackish for prolonged periods as he pushes farther and farther out of the nest and bites anything that passes by. If what he so grabs is edible, he swallows it; if it happens to be a rival, he carries him some distance from the nest and dumps him. The extreme aggressiveness of bullheads at such

Male river bullhead grabbing female to pull her into his cave

times was demonstrated by one individual, who dashed fifteen inches across the tank to grab another male who was not even headed in his direction, carried him four times around the tank, and then viciously spat him out in a far corner.

Sooner or later, however, the fish he bites is a female, and then the male has attained his goal, for she is sexually stimulated by the bite which engulfs her entire head and neck.

The most common courtship procedure as observed so far seems to begin when the waiting male nods his head with short, jerky motions as the female approaches. Then he darts forward to grab her in the manner described above. He may hold on to his bride while he backs into the nesting cave, or he may release her. If she is ready to spawn, she will indicate this by flattening her fins and lowering her head, and then follow the male into the cave. Once inside, she is further courted by her suitor, who now erects his fins and again nods vigorously. Soon after, the female turns upside-down for an inspection of the roof, and then, satisfied that everything is as it should be, she wastes no more time in depositing her batch of eggs. The male has moved over to leave her enough room, but as she lays her eggs, he moves back and positions himself directly beneath her, and fertilizes the eggs as they are laid. Then the female leaves, and the male begins his guard duty. Two females may lay their eggs into the same nest at the same time without causing any fighting or commotion.

From that point on, the male guards and fans the eggs

without interruption. He is still just as aggressive as before, and darts out to bite anything that moves even if it happens to be some distance from the nest. The courage and fearlessness with which these small fish attack even large animals that appear to threaten their offspring are remarkable, and have drawn the admiring comments of observers for more than a century.

For almost four weeks following the fertilization of the eggs the male never slackens in his devotion to duty. The constant vigorous fanning seems to be necessary for a normal development of the eggs, and he never seems to tire to the point where he will stop for more than a few minutes. On the other hand, he never inspects the eggs as many other fish parents do; it was observed that those that spoil are swept away by the current caused by the fanning.

Except for short sorties to grab some conveniently passing prey, the father does not leave his post. Towards the end of the four-week incubation period, he can be observed tilting his head to look at the eggs. Apparently he knows instinctively that the long wait is almost over, for invariably the eggs hatch a few days after he has eyed them for the first time.

So far, observing the newly-hatched young has been difficult, because they immediately retire into the darkest corner of the nesting cave in what seems to be an instinctive reaction to light. In the studies made so far, young bullheads left in the tank after hatching were eaten by the father; this was undoubtedly a result of the artificial environment from which some important ingredient was

With unprecedented fury, a male river bullhead chases an intruder

*The male faithfully fans
and guards the eggs*

missing. It is believed that, under normal conditions, the bullhead father behaves very much like the male stickleback, who guards the young after hatching. It remains for future observers to provide an environment that permits the successful raising of a brood, and the discovery of just where and how the father's care for his offspring is terminated. However that may be, the entertaining habits of the river bullhead and its fearlessness while guarding its nest make this comical-looking little fish a rewarding object of study for any aquarium hobbyist.

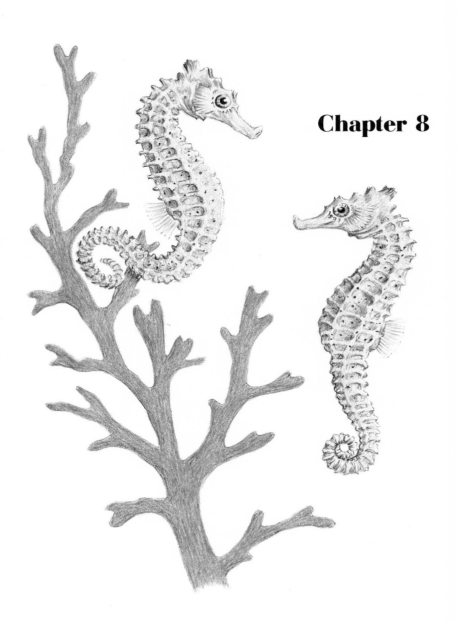

Chapter 8

SEA HORSES
The Pregnant Fathers

THE SMALL, strange creatures with their horse-shaped heads and bony bodies, looking oddly like the "knights" in a chess game, bobbed and circled about in the water of the tank, two unlikely little mermaids performing an exotic underwater ballet. Their tails curled and uncurled as they moved up and down, their fins were a blur of motion. The courtship dance—for that was the meaning of the strange ritual—continued as the male wooed the female in an age-old performance and she responded. As they danced, they moved closer and closer to one another, until finally their bodies intertwined. At that point, the female inserted her ovipositor into a slit in the pouch visible on the male's belly, and deposited her eggs inside. As soon as she had completed her spawning, she disengaged herself from the male and swam off. A short distance away, she gripped the branch of a water plant with her prehensile tail, and remained motionless, waiting for some small edible creature to appear. Her partner of just a few minutes ago was left alone, totally ignored, for along with the eggs, she had passed on to her mate the sole responsibility for their future offspring.

Over the next days and weeks, the "pregnant" male displayed all the symptoms of a condition normally reserved exclusively for the females of the most advanced groups in the entire animal kingdom. As the eggs in the pouch developed, it became steadily more distended, until the male's balance was impaired and unrestricted movement became difficult. That, however, was no great drawback for the pregnant father; sea horses normally do not swim about much, preferring instead to cling to plants or other protuberances for support, and waiting patiently for tiny aquatic organisms to pass by close enough to be snapped up.

Sea horses belong to a peculiar group of bony fishes gathered in the suborder of *Lophobranchiata*, which includes the so-called sea needles or pipefish. These slender, greatly-elongated fish swim horizontally, but often move about or rest in a vertical position, sometimes head-up,

A pigmy sea horse, life-size

*A so-called sea dragon, bizarre-looking
close relative of the sea horses*

sometimes head-down, where they may have a striking resemblance to aquatic plants, especially because they can adapt their coloring to their background. Although they look so different, they are not only closely related to the sea horses but also have very similar courtship and breeding habits.

The scientific name of the suborder refers to the structure of their gills, which consist of tufts instead of being comb-like as in most other species of fish. The armor of sea horses, which is a kind of skin-skeleton made up of dozens of bony rings—usually more than fifty—that encircle the body from neck to tail, and are distinguished by numerous protuberances, offers them protection against certain enemies.

Most sea horses are small, averaging between three and seven inches in length, of which half is taken up by the tail. The largest, which occur in the Pacific, usually measure about a foot, although individual specimens almost twenty inches long have been found in the Australian seas and near Japan. The majority of sea horses prefer the warmer oceans; some, however, live in the relatively cold waters of the Atlantic north to Cape Cod, and in the English Channel.

Certain exotic members of the group are especially fascinating to look at, having most peculiar body shapes and appendages that makes some of them resemble miniature dragons, and they are in fact known as "sea dragons" in the regions where they occur.

Like many other fish, sea horses and their relatives are capable of extensive color changes, and can adjust their coloring and pattern to conform to that of their surroundings. Although this calls for greenish or brownish hues in most cases, background coloration may induce a sea horse to turn blackish, bright red, yellow, or even silvery as the occasion demands it. Spotted and mottled patterns also are common.

The most conspicuous difference between the habits of a sea horse and those of other fish is its way of moving about in the water, for it swims always in a vertical position. The tail has no fins, and is not used for propelling, only for gripping and holding on to any convenient support. Sea horses thus have the distinction of being the only fish with a prehensile tail.

Maintaining the vertical swimming position and the equilibrium this requires while moving about is accom-

A common sea horse that has changed its color to adapt to red algae

plished with the help of the pectoral fins, which can be moved so rapidly that they appear only as a blur as the little animal darts back and forth in the water. It never attempts to swim great distances, and usually stays within a rather limited territory. If it wishes to descend, the sea horse curves its neck forward and rolls its tail into a tight coil; ascent is achieved by straightening out the body and tail.

Both the coloring and the swimming position of a sea horse are indicators of health; if the fish pales—except in a light-colored environment to which it tries to adapt—and swims tilted on one side, it is sick, and unfortunately usually beyond help.

As could be expected in a creature whose livelihood depends upon finding tiny and often minute organisms, sea horses have very keen vision, as anyone will confirm after watching them dart out to grab minute and all but invisible prey. Their large eyes can be moved independently, like those of a chameleon, which for practical purposes means that they can follow the progress of one victim with one eye, while watching another prey coming from a different direction with the other eye without having to change their position.

All these peculiar and distinctive features, however, pale into insignificance when compared to their unique breeding habits, which up until the middle of the last century were completely misinterpreted. In a book on fish published in Europe just a hundred years ago, the author states that "considerable argument" then still existed about

*A pair of sea horses just
prior to mating*

the sea horses' manner of reproduction, but that it appeared that the eggs were "attached externally" to the male's body. It is hardly surprising that older naturalists, while observing the strange mating behavior of these little fish, were convinced that the pouched individuals were females, and that the process they were witnessing was a transferral of sperm rather than the depositing of the eggs. When the full facts were finally established, the story of the pregnant fathers caused considerable excitement.

More interesting than any other aspect of this unusual mode of reproduction is the fact that the males go through a very real pregnancy; the pouch is not just a receptacle in which the eggs are kept until they hatch. Located under the pelvic bone, the pouch is joined in the middle, and has a slot-like opening. Except during the breeding period, it is not conspicuous, and the slot hardly visible.

When mating occurs, the female inserts her ovipositor into the slot and injects her eggs, which may number some two hundred, into the pouch. As they pass into the main compartment, they are fertilized. Once the eggs are inside, the tissues of the pouch walls undergo great changes. They swell, grow, and acquire a sponge-like structure. The capillary blood vessels multiply. In effect, placentation similar to that known in female mammals during pregnancy occurs. The eggs are engulfed by compartments in the tissues of the pouch walls.

During the following days and weeks, the initially tiny eggs grow and take up more and more tissue. Those that cannot find a suitable spot to adhere to degenerate and die. These changes are heralded externally by the visible enlargement of the pouch.

After a period of time that may vary with the circumstances, the skin of each egg splits, and the embryo now rests, embedded in the pouch tissue, until it has used up all its egg yolk. Finally, approximately forty to fifty days after fertilization, the birth of the fully formed young begins.

A "pregnant" male sea horse

Male sea horse giving birth to fully developed young

Giving birth is not easy for the male, and quite evidently causes him great discomfort and distress, judging from his behavior. In many cases, the male can be observed as he writhes and struggles on the bottom in his efforts to eject the young from the pouch. As the babies appear in increasing numbers, the contractions become less violent, and the pouch shrinks, until finally the last of the young sea horses have seen the light of the day. At that point, the pouch is completely deflated, and the slot opening closes to leave only a thin line. Soon, the tissues will assume their normal structure and the number of blood vessels in the pouch walls will decline as the last traces of the male's pregnancy vanish.

Premature births are not rare among sea horses; in such cases, the young are ejected from the pouch with portions of their yolk sacs still adhering to their bodies. This is a serious handicap, and for such prematurely-born offspring, the prognosis for survival until adulthood is almost nil. In the majority of cases, however, the young sea horses are born fully formed, which gives them a much better chance to survive beyond the first few days of their lives.

In the beginning, sea horse offspring do not resemble their parents; they certainly are not, as some would have

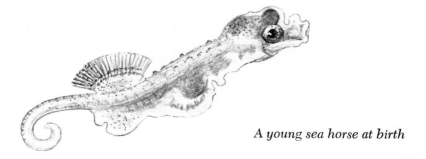

A young sea horse at birth

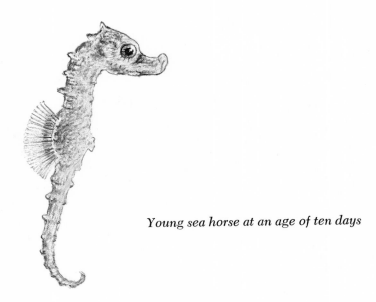

Young sea horse at an age of ten days

it, miniature adults. For one thing, they have not yet acquired the capacity for swimming in a vertical position; during the first week, they swim horizontally like other fish. For another, they are almost transparent and without pigmentation; they appear to be all eyes, and their short, pug-like snouts lend them a rather comical expression. Only after a week or so do they begin to look very much like the adults: they swim upright, the snout has lengthened, and pigmentation has increased.

From the moment of their birth, the young sea horses are on their own. Once the babies have been ejected from his pouch, the father's task is done, and he ignores his offspring even though the water around him may teem with them. The strange "male birth" has completed one of the most unusual breeding cycles in the animal kingdom.

Guide to the Care of Fish Described in This Book

WITH THE possible exception of such locally available species as sticklebacks, the fish described in this book are not good subjects for the efforts of a novice aquarist. It takes quite a bit of experience to attempt the raising and breeding of species such as the discus or the jewel fish. Nor is the book intended to be a handbook on how to keep an aquarium: there are many excellent and relatively inexpensive publications on sale in pet shops and book stores that give extensive information to those who plan to get interested in setting up and maintaining an aquarium, and become devotees of this fascinating hobby.

For the aquarist with some experience, however, who has the wish to observe, in his own tank, the unusual and entertaining behavior displayed by these fish during the mating season, a few guidelines and tips have been provided in the pages that follow, together with some basic data about the fish themselves. As a ground rule, it is always best to provide a separate tank for a breeding pair, because it can be equipped individually to suit the requirements of each species; also, observation of the courtship and mating activities is much easier in an uncrowded tank.

SPRAYING CHARACIN *(Copeina arnoldi)*

A peaceful and attractive species about 3 inches long. It is not particularly difficult to keep, but cannot easily be induced to breed. Because of their habit of depositing the eggs out of water, plants or floating pieces of wood have to be provided for the breeding pair. The water has to be soft and slightly acid, the temperature approximately 75 degrees. The tank should be large, no less than 15-gallon capacity, and planted preferably with a few broad-leaved plants. After the eggs have hatched and the young fry have been washed down into the water by the male, the parents should be removed, and the young fed with very fine live food.

SUCKERMOUTH CATFISH *(Loricaria filamentosa)*

The problem with these fish is to supply them with sufficient vegetable material, because that is their sole food. The average aquarium does not have enough algae to satisfy their appetite, and their diet is best supplemented with portions of boiled spinach, on which they seem to thrive. Temperature and water acidity are not very important factors with suckermouths, water temperatures ranging from 70-78 degrees being acceptable. These 8-inch fish have been succesfully bred in captivity, and require a well-planted tank with several large stones. The parents should be left in the tank for several days after the eggs hatch because the male guards the young.

BITTERLING *(Rhodeus amarus)*

A well-planted aquarium with relatively cold water (65 degrees) is prefered by this tiny, 2-inch European species. It will breed in captivity if the tank is not too small, well-planted, and several live fresh-water mussels have been placed into the tank so the female can deposit her eggs. After the young have been ejected by the mussel, parents and offspring should be separated. Bitterlings are not demanding but need live food at intervals.

DOGFISH *(Umbra krameri)*

A densely planted aquarium is needed for this interesting and lively little fish if it is to breed successfully. The female, who with a length of 5 inches is considerably larger than the 3½-inch male, builds a well-hidden nest. Water conditions—acidity and temperature—are not very important factors, as long as the latter does not go much above 70 degrees. Any kind of food accepted by other small fish of temperate regions is suitable, although live food is preferred.

NEON GOBY *(Elacatinus oceanops)*

These beautiful little fish are a wonderful addition to any marine aquarium that does not contain other fish large and quarrelsome enough to bother the gobies, which attain a maximum length of only 3 inches.

The neon goby is one of the few marine fish that have been bred successfully in captivity. For maximum breeding conditions, the gobies should be separated from other fish in a breeding tank and supplied with several large, smooth shells, which they can use as convenient nesting sites.

The newly-hatched young, which are tiny, should not be separated from their parents. Neon gobies protect their offspring for several days after they hatch, and normally there is no danger of the small fry being attacked by their parents.

Feeding should follow along the lines of other small marine fish; for the young, infusorians and plankton are necessary during the initial period.

MUDSKIPPER *(Periophthalmus koelreuteri)*

This fascinating 6-inch fish needs a special environment that is half aquarium, half terrarium. Mudskippers are very hardy and not at all choosy about the type of water available, for they can live in fresh, brackish, and salt water without suffering ill effects. The temperature, however, has to be fairly high—about 75 degrees—and the air in the tank warm and humid, because they spend so much time out of the water. The terrarium part should be arranged with some stones and sand extending beach-like out of the water, so that the mudskipper can climb up and bask on a look-out point. They accept both live and dead food, which they like to eat on land.

RAINBOW WRASSE *(Coris julis)*

A hardy, attractive species from the Mediterranean, and well suited to a large salt-water aquarium, for it grows to a length of 8 inches. Males quarrel among themselves, but usually not with other fish. Breeding attempts are made difficult by the fact that all of these wrasses start life as females and only later change to males, and the difference in color patterns, although often indicative of a sex change, is not a reliable indicator. Care and feeding of the rainbow wrasse is similar to that of other inhabitants of a salt-water aquarium.

DISCUS FISH *(Symphysodon sp.)*

All the members of this genus are relatively difficult to keep, and very difficult to breed. They should not be kept with other fish even though they are not aggressive. The common discus needs an even larger tank than the 5-inch blue discus. Their tanks should be densely planted because they are nervous and shy and need hiding places. Care has to be exercised when approaching these fish, for they panic easily and may hurt themselves badly if they do. One portion of the tank should be dimly lit so they can hide when they are nervous.

Water conditions are important; hardness should not exceed 5 DH, and the temperature should not be less than 75 degrees. For successful spawning, the water of the breeding tank requires a pH of 5.5–6.0. A mated pair has to be supplied with a smooth tile, stone, or piece of slate that has been well-cleaned and placed slanted against a wall of the tank. If the eggs are successfully hatched, no attempt should be made to remove the young until they are at least half an inch long and ready to take live food such as baby brine shrimp and sifted *Daphnia*. Determining sex is difficult; when the fish are about 4 or 5 inches long, they should be observed to see which pair off naturally. Such a pair can then be removed to a breeding tank with a capacity of no less than 15 gallons.

JEWEL FISH (RUBY CICHLID) *(Hemichromis bimaculatus)*

Extremely beautiful but so aggressive that they have to be kept in a tank of their own, which should have a capacity of at least fifteen gallons, even when they are not breeding. The aquarium should not be planted, because these fish will uproot any plant. Only artificial plants firmly anchored to the bottom of the tank have a chance of remaining fixed, and may be used if greenery is desired as ornamentation.

Jewel fish are hardy and do not require any special care; the water conditions and food suitable for other cichlids of comparable size are acceptable to jewel fish. As with the others, variety in the diet is important, especially because a well-balanced diet brings out the best color in the fish.

For breeding, the water temperature should be approximately 77–78 degrees. Jewel fish are devoted and utterly fearless, and will bite anything and anybody that appears to threaten their brood, including a human hand that is lowered into the water.

Once the young are large enough to be separated from the adults, their care is similar to that of other cichlid small fry.

Mozambique Mouthbrooder *(Tilapia mossambica)*

Because of their large size—they may attain a length of 14 inches—these fish have to be kept in a separate tank, which should be of a 15–20-gallon capacity, and densely planted, especially if they are expected to breed. They are hearty eaters, and accept any type of food suitable for other cichlids of their size.

For breeding, the water temperature should be around 78 degrees; the degree of water hardness is not an especially important factor. The bottom of the tank should be covered with gravel to a depth of several inches so that the male can dig its deep nest pit.

As soon as the male has fertilized the eggs, he should be removed from the tank. The female has to be in prime condition because she does not eat during the almost two weeks she carries the eggs in her mouth. The newly-hatched young can be fed with baby brine shrimp and *Daphnia*. They should be left with the mother during the first days after they are free-swimming because they seek shelter in her mouth at this stage.

Betta (Siamese Fighting Fish) *(Betta splendens)*

These beautiful and showy fish are comparatively hardy but short-lived, with a life span that rarely exceeds two years. Because of their fighting instincts, males cannot be kept together in a tank, but one male and several females may be kept in a community tank without difficulty.

For breeding, they should be separated, with the male having the run of the aquarium, while the female is segregated in a floating jar just inside the tank where the male can see but not touch her.

The breeding tank does not have to be very large, and should be filled with no more than about 6 inches of water registering a temperature of approximately 84 degrees. The water condition for bettas is not very important, for they are rather robust and adaptable to varying degrees of hardness, but water with a pH of between 6.7 and 7.3 seems to be best.

The male should be permitted to build his bubble nest before the female is released from her jar. After spawning is completed, immediate removal of the female is recommended, because the male may otherwise hurt or even kill her.

As soon as the young can swim freely, the male also should be removed, and the tiny fry have to be fed with live food, the best being either infusoria collected from a pond, if that is feasible, or prepared from tablets available at pet shops. Hard-boiled mashed egg yolk is also a good food, which should be fed in small quantities two or three times a day. All uneaten food should be promptly removed because the young fish are especially susceptible to fouled water.

When the hatchlings are about six days old, they can be

fed on live baby brine shrimp, which have to be washed to remove excess salt.

After about two months, sex determination can be made from fin size and shape, and young males should be separated because they otherwise will start to fight. At an age of between four and six months, bettas have attained their adult size of 2½ inches and are in their prime for breeding purposes.

THREE-SPINED STICKLEBACK *(Gasterosteus aculeatus)*

These fish may be difficult to obtain in pet shops, which tend to deal almost exclusively in exotic species, but can be found in many different types of streams, ponds, and lakes. It is best to keep them in a separate tank if they are to be bred, with perhaps one male and two or three females to each tank. Introducing other males into the aquarium at breeding time usually leads to exhausting and fruitless battles; only in a large tank will two males find sufficient territory to build nests.

The tank should be planted to a reasonable density, and spare plants with small leaves and lots of roots should be added as nesting material for the male.

Sticklebacks are hardy and easy to feed. Water conditions are not an important factor; temperatures should be around 70 degrees. Food ranging from fish eggs to aquatic insects and fish small enough to swallow is acceptable. So is the standard dried food available at pet stores if it is alternated with live food. An occasional treat of tubifex worms or fresh brine shrimp is recommended.

RIVER BULLHEAD *(Cottus gobio)*

River bullheads have to be kept in a separate tank for breeding, but even at other times they are really not suitable for a community tank containing smaller fish. As the wide head and large mouth indicate, the 5-inch bullhead will eat anything it can swallow, and is not choosy. The breeding tank can be planted, and should have a thick layer of sand, and one or two large curved pieces of broken flowerpot or concave stone arranged to form a cave in the sand as shown in the illustrations on pp. 112-124. Such artificial "caves" have to be well-anchored so the bullhead's digging will not cause them to collapse.

Water conditions are no problem in this case, for the river bullhead can adapt to a fairly wide range of acidity and temperature, the latter being acceptable at anything from 67 to 72 degrees.

Although they can be trained to accept food such as pieces of fish or meat, live food ranging from aquatic insect larvae and earthworms to small fish are preferable.

SEA HORSE *(Hippocampus sp.)*

Extremely interesting to observe, but not easy to keep, sea horses require knowledge of optimum conditions for a salt-water aquarium. They are very peaceful toward other fish, and can therefore be kept without difficulty in a community tank. Live food is necessary if they are to survive over any length of time, and especially if breeding is attempted. Fairy shrimp and other small crustaceans are the best type of food.

For breeding, sea horses are preferably kept in a separate tank, where their fascinating mating habits can be observed without interruption, and where the young are safe from other fish.

Raising the small fry is difficult because they demand live food of a very small size, preferably marine plankton. However, care and patience has its rewards, for these small, odd-looking fish are among the most interesting inhabitants any salt-water aquarium can have.

Scientific Names and Geographic Range

Anabantidae (Labyrinth Fish) Tropical Asia and Africa

Betta splendens (Betta or Siamese Fighting Fish) Malay Peninsula and Thailand

Carrassius auratus (Goldfish) Asia and Eastern Europe

Cichlidae (Cichlids) American and Old World tropics

Copeina arnoldi (Spraying Characin) Lower Amazon region

Coris julis (Rainbow Wrasse) Mediterranean Sea

Cottus bairdi (Muddler) North American Atlantic coastal regions

Cottus gobio (River Bullhead) Northern and Central Europe

Elacatinus oceanops (Neon Goby) West Indies

Gasterosteus aculeatus (Three-spined Stickleback) Europe and North America

Gasterosteus pungitius (Nine-spined Stickleback) Europe and North America

Gasterosteus spinachia (Fifteen-spined Stickleback) North European coastal regions

Haplochromis multicolor (Small or Egyptian Mouthbrooder) East Africa and Egypt

Hemichromis bimaculatus (Jewel Fish, Ruby or Red Cichlid) Northern tropical Africa

Hemichromis fasciatus (Banded or Angolan Jewel Fish) Northwestern tropical Africa

Hippocampus kuda (Yellow or Golden Sea Horse) Indo-Pacific Ocean

Hippocampus zosterae (Pigmy Sea Horse) West Indies and Gulf of Mexico

Loricaria filamentosa (Suckermouth Catfish) Northern South America

Periophthalmus koelreuteri (Mudskipper) Old World tropical coastal regions

Phyllopteryx eques (Sea Dragon) Australo-Pacific Ocean

Pterophyllum scalare (Angelfish or Scalare) Amazon regions and Guiana

Rhodeus amarus (Bitterling) Central Europe and Eurasia

Symphysodon aequifasciata haraldi (Blue Discus) Amazon region

Symphysodon discus (Common Discus) Amazon, Rio Negro, and Rio Cuprai regions of Brazil

Tilapia macrocephala (Black-chinned Mouthbrooder) Northeast Africa

Tilapia mossambica (Mozambique Mouthbrooder) East Africa

Umbra krameri (Dogfish) Central Europe

Bibliography

Atz, James W. and Douglas Faulkner. *Aquarium Fishes.* The Viking Press, 1971.

Axelrod, Herbert A. and William Vorderwinkler. *Encyclopedia of Tropical Fishes.* TFH Publications, 1968.

Coates, Christopher W. *Tropical Fishes as Pets.* Macmillan Company, 1961.

Lorenz, Konrad. *Tiergeschichten.* Verlag Dr. G. Borotha-Schoeler, 1971.

Schiotz, Arne, and Preben Dahlstrom. *A Guide to Aquarium Fishes and Plants.* Willam Collins Sons & Co. Ltd., and J. B. Lippincott Company, 1972.

Schwartz, Elisabeth. *Fische Hinter Glass.* Altberliner Verlag Lucie Grosser, 1951.

Timmerman, G. J. M. and Gene Wolfsheimer. *Color Guide to Tropical Fish.* Sterling Publishing Co., 1959.

Index

Pages on which illustrations appear are shown in *italics*.